HUMAN RIGHTS IN NORTH KOREA: CHALLENGES AND OPPORTUNITIES

HEARING

BEFORE THE

SUBCOMMITTEE ON AFRICA, GLOBAL HEALTH, AND HUMAN RIGHTS

OF THE

COMMITTEE ON FOREIGN AFFAIRS
HOUSE OF REPRESENTATIVES

ONE HUNDRED TWELFTH CONGRESS

FIRST SESSION

SEPTEMBER 20, 2011

Serial No. 112–104

Printed for the use of the Committee on Foreign Affairs

Available via the World Wide Web: http://www.foreignaffairs.house.gov/

U.S. GOVERNMENT PRINTING OFFICE

68–443PDF   WASHINGTON : 2011

For sale by the Superintendent of Documents, U.S. Government Printing Office
Internet: bookstore.gpo.gov   Phone: toll free (866) 512–1800; DC area (202) 512–1800
Fax: (202) 512–2104   Mail: Stop IDCC, Washington, DC 20402–0001

COMMITTEE ON FOREIGN AFFAIRS

ILEANA ROS-LEHTINEN, Florida, *Chairman*

CHRISTOPHER H. SMITH, New Jersey
DAN BURTON, Indiana
ELTON GALLEGLY, California
DANA ROHRABACHER, California
DONALD A. MANZULLO, Illinois
EDWARD R. ROYCE, California
STEVE CHABOT, Ohio
RON PAUL, Texas
MIKE PENCE, Indiana
JOE WILSON, South Carolina
CONNIE MACK, Florida
JEFF FORTENBERRY, Nebraska
MICHAEL T. McCAUL, Texas
TED POE, Texas
GUS M. BILIRAKIS, Florida
JEAN SCHMIDT, Ohio
BILL JOHNSON, Ohio
DAVID RIVERA, Florida
MIKE KELLY, Pennsylvania
TIM GRIFFIN, Arkansas
TOM MARINO, Pennsylvania
JEFF DUNCAN, South Carolina
ANN MARIE BUERKLE, New York
RENEE ELLMERS, North Carolina
VACANT

HOWARD L. BERMAN, California
GARY L. ACKERMAN, New York
ENI F.H. FALEOMAVAEGA, American Samoa
DONALD M. PAYNE, New Jersey
BRAD SHERMAN, California
ELIOT L. ENGEL, New York
GREGORY W. MEEKS, New York
RUSS CARNAHAN, Missouri
ALBIO SIRES, New Jersey
GERALD E. CONNOLLY, Virginia
THEODORE E. DEUTCH, Florida
DENNIS CARDOZA, California
BEN CHANDLER, Kentucky
BRIAN HIGGINS, New York
ALLYSON SCHWARTZ, Pennsylvania
CHRISTOPHER S. MURPHY, Connecticut
FREDERICA WILSON, Florida
KAREN BASS, California
WILLIAM KEATING, Massachusetts
DAVID CICILLINE, Rhode Island

YLEEM D.S. POBLETE, *Staff Director*
RICHARD J. KESSLER, *Democratic Staff Director*

———

SUBCOMMITTEE ON AFRICA, GLOBAL HEALTH, AND HUMAN RIGHTS

CHRISTOPHER H. SMITH, New Jersey, *Chairman*

JEFF FORTENBERRY, Nebraska
TIM GRIFFIN, Arkansas
TOM MARINO, Pennsylvania
ANN MARIE BUERKLE, New York

DONALD M. PAYNE, New Jersey
KAREN BASS, California
RUSS CARNAHAN, Missouri

CONTENTS

HUMAN RIGHTS IN NORTH KOREA: CHALLENGES AND OPPORTUNITIES

TUESDAY, SEPTEMBER 20, 2011

HOUSE OF REPRESENTATIVES,
SUBCOMMITTEE ON AFRICA, GLOBAL HEALTH,
AND HUMAN RIGHTS
COMMITTEE ON FOREIGN AFFAIRS,
Washington, DC.

The subcommittee met, pursuant to notice, at 3 o'clock p.m., in room 2172, Rayburn House Office Building, Hon. Christopher H. Smith (chairman of the subcommittee) presiding.

Mr. SMITH. The subcommittee will come to order. And good afternoon to everybody. I want to thank you for joining us for this very important hearing to examine a country with one of the worst human rights records in the entire world. The Democratic People's Republic of Korea is known to be the world's most isolated country as its citizens are prohibited from traveling either internally or internationally without express permission. Communications with the outside world are also tightly regulated in attempts by the dictatorship to filter all information accessible by the North Korean people.

Therefore, the testimony to be provided today by our distinguished panel, and in particular our two defector witnesses, is particularly welcomed and appreciated. Mrs. Kim Young Soon and Mrs. Kim Hye Sook, who both have survived the extreme deprivations of the North Korean prison camps, have traveled all the way from South Korea to share their experiences with our subcommittee. On behalf of the subcommittee, I want to thank them and convey to them our sincerest gratitude.

I also want to thank Suzanne Scholte for her extraordinary work over these many years. I have chaired several hearings on North Korean human rights, and in every one of those hearings she has played a critical part in helping us to get witnesses who tell the true unvarnished story of what is actually happening in North Korea. Our two witnesses will tell the story and they will be speaking on behalf of an estimated 150,000 to 200,000 prisoners currently held in North Korean labor camps.

It is our hope that their testimony will help to galvanize the international community to take action to secure the freedom of those who are needlessly suffering and dying under truly horrific conditions. Those living in the prison camps are not the only ones suffering in North Korea. As one of our witnesses—again, Suzanne Scholte—will testify, in North Korea every single human right en-

(1)

shrined in the Universal Declaration on Human Rights is violated and it is often violated with absolute impunity.

North Korea is listed by the State Department as a Tier III country with respect to human trafficking. In other words, they are egregious violators of modern-day slavery, buying and selling women and others as a commodity.

North Korea was also just designated this month as one of eight Countries of Particular Concern for its violations of religious freedom.

But not all the testimony during this hearing will be bleak, although much of it will be. We will hear about the new potential for communication to and with the North Korean people and explore possibilities for peaceful change given upcoming political events in North Korea and changes in other countries in the region. We look forward to discussing this potential to improve the lives of all people living in North Korea.

I would like to now introduce our very distinguished panel and again thank all of you for being here today. I also want to thank C–SPAN for being here, for taking this information and conveying it to the American people. North Korea, because it is so closed, very often evades all scrutiny, so people know about it but don't know very much. Your testimony, again, will help to shatter that lackadaisical sense of what Americans know and think about North Korea, so thank you again.

We will begin with Ms. Suzanne Scholte who is the president of the Defense Forum Foundation and is a leader of several groups focused on protecting human rights in North Korea. She was recognized in 2010 with the Walter Judd Freedom Award, and in 2008 with the Seoul Peace Prize. Ms. Scholte has helped rescue hundreds of North Korean refugees and facilitated the travel of defectors to speak in the United States. She has participated in numerous congressional hearings on North Korea on a wide range of topics, including political prison camps, trafficking of North Korean women, religious persecution, and North Korean refugees in China.

I would note parenthetically that when we held a hearing on trafficked women, some of the—what they thought were lucky women who got out of North Korea into China—Ms. Scholte actually brought to this committee women who—one woman who went after her daughter, who made her way into China only to be sold into slavery, and then she and her daughter who went looking to rescue the trafficked women were themselves sold into sexual slavery.

We will then hear from Ms. Kim Young Soon, Committee for the Democratization of North Korea, and she was a dancer and an actress in the North Korean Army. She was arrested in 1970 and sent to the Yoduk political prison camp with members of her family. Her parents and eldest son died in the camp, and her husband and youngest son later died trying to escape North Korea. Ms. Kim eventually escaped and has dedicated her life to exposing the truth about the hideous prison camps in North Korea by sharing her story around the globe. She is an outspoken defector, serving as the vice president of the Committee for the Democratization of North Korea and other human rights advocacy groups.

We will then hear from Ms. Kim Hye Sook, who is a survivor of nearly three decades in Bukchang political prison camp. She and her family were imprisoned for "guilt by association" because of her grandfather's defection to South Korea. She was just 13 years old. Ms. Kim regularly witnessed executions and abuse and endured manual labor, constant hunger, and the deaths of several family members. Once released, she fled to China but was forced to return to North Korea by her employer, where she was arrested again. When she escaped she returned to China but was sold by human traffickers, again like the other witnesses we have had before this committee.

She eventually escaped to South Korea and continues to tell her story around the world. Earlier this year she published her memoirs in a book entitled, "A Concentration Camp Retold in Tears."

We will then hear from Mr. Greg Scarlatoiu, Committee for Human Rights in North Korea. Mr. Scarlatoiu is the executive director of the Committee for Human Rights in North Korea, which was established to focus world attention on human rights abuses in North Korea and to offer creative solutions. Born and raised in Romania, he was a Bucharest University freshman when he witnessed the fall of Communism in eastern Europe, Nicolae Ceausescu's barbaric regime.

He lived in South Korea for 10 years and has authored English and Korean language articles on the applicability of the eastern European experience to North Korea context, as well as a weekly Korean language broadcast into North Korea by Radio Free Asia, and we welcome him as well.

I would like to now yield to my friend and colleague Mr. Payne for any opening comments he might have.

Mr. PAYNE. Thank you very much, Mr. Chairman, for calling this very important hearing. And I would like to certainly express my appreciation to the witnesses here who have agreed to testify. Each of your stories help us to better understand the extent and magnitude of the human rights abuses of North Korea, and your guidance will help us to target our efforts in alleviating some of these terrible injustices.

Human rights violations in North Korea are among the worst in the world. Under Kim Jong Il's regime, North Korean citizens regularly face extra judiciary killings and detentions for basic political expressions, seemingly ordinary market activities, or unauthorized domestic travel. North Korea doesn't seem to even need to violate the regime's rules themselves, since they can be penalized for even the actions not of themselves but actually of their families, which is certainly unfair and unjust.

While many of us cannot imagine a more stifling human rights environment, according to some observers, the conditions are worsening due to the preparation for Jong Il's son, Kim Jong Un, to take over.

In 2004 Congress passed a North Korean Human Rights Act authorizing funds toward human rights efforts and improving the flow of information to North Korea. Currently this amounts to $2 million annually for human rights and democracy, $2 million for freedom of information programs and $20 million to assist North Korean refugees. I am interested in hearing from the panelists who have expertise in that area about their views on how proposed cuts to our international affairs budget would impact on our ability to adequately continue to fund these programs that have been successful in getting information to date.

Although it is not in the realm of your testimony necessarily, I was very disturbed at the behavior of the North Korean leadership in November 2010 when it attacked South Korea's island of Yeonpyeong with artillery shells, killing several people. This irresponsible behavior of government really is unwarranted and really needs to have continued watching and scrutinizing as to their behavior. Also their continued adventurism into ballistic missiles and other weapons of war certainly disturb us.

So I certainly look forward to your testimonies, and thank you again for your willingness to share them. And I yield back the balance of my time.

Mr. SMITH. Thank you very much.

Would either of my other colleagues like to—no.

I would like to now then yield the floor for such time as she may consume to Ms. Scholte. Let me, before you start, make a point. We also invited Ambassador-at-Large King, who could not be here because he is out of the country. He wanted to be here, and said very clearly he would gladly come and testify at a later date. And he also wanted to provide the testimony with a closed briefing as well on recent events, including the human rights situation in North Korea.

Bob King, as my colleagues know so well, especially Mr. Payne, was the chief of staff for the Foreign Affairs Committee and very good choice for Ambassador, so we look forward to hearing from him as well. So, Ms. Scholte.

STATEMENT OF MS. SUZANNE SCHOLTE, PRESIDENT, DEFENSE FORUM FOUNDATION

Ms. SCHOLTE. Well, first of all, I just want to thank Congressman Smith for your many years of devotion on the North Korea human rights issues. And I want to thank Congressman Payne as well. It has been an honor and pleasure to work with your staff on our shared love for the Sahrawi people of Western Sahara, another divided country that is trying to get their freedom through self-determination.

I want to give two main points at this hearing today. First of all, North Korea continues to be one of the darkest places on earth, yet we fail to focus on the main issue, which is the human rights issues, because we have instead focused on the nuclear issue, and this has had tragic results.

Second, despite this ongoing tragedy, there is hope because of changes that are happening in that country. But if we fail to enact the policies that address the human rights conditions and empower those who can bring about change, then we will certainly end up just prolonging this regime.

While we witness people rising up in North Africa, in the Middle East, we wonder why do North Koreans, who are arguably the most persecuted people in the world, not rise up? It is precisely because they are the most persecuted in the world. North Koreans are the only people in the world that do not enjoy one single human right that is enshrined in the Universal Declaration of Human Rights, a document, ironically, that was adopted in 1948, the same year that Kim Il Sung came to power. This declaration was in response to the atrocities committed by the Axis powers during World War II.

When the Nazi death camps were liberated by the Allied Forces during that war, the international community vowed never again, never again would we allow these kinds of atrocities to occur. But the political prison camps in North Korea have existed longer than the Soviet gulag, longer than the Chinese Laogai, and longer than the Nazi death camps.

Your two defector witnesses today are living proof of the horrors of these camps, as well as the length of their existence. One was imprisoned in Yoduk in the 1970s, while another was imprisoned for 28 years, up through the beginning of this decade, in Bukchang. We have seen millions of North Koreans starve to death despite billions of economic assistance.

And North Koreans are not the only ones who suffer from Kim Jong Il's dictatorship. But South Korean POWs are still being held in North Korea today, while at least 108,308 captives are being held in North Korea, including 80,000 abductees from South Korea and hundreds of others from 13 countries, as recently documented by the Committee for Human Rights in North Korea.

Former Presidents Bill Clinton and George Bush made human rights a secondary issue, with the hope of engaging North Korea to give up their nuclear ambitions. We see the failure of these efforts as North Korea has realized its nuclear ambitions and its proliferation activity continues. Kim Jong Il may be an evil dictator, but he has brilliantly manipulated the good intentions of both America and South Korea.

My second point: There is hope because things are changing in North Korea. Despite Kim Jong Il's best efforts to literally keep North Koreans in the dark, up to 60 percent of North Koreans have access to some form of information beyond the regime's propaganda. They are increasingly learning that the source of their misery is not America or South Korea, as they are brainwashed from childhood to believe, but the source of their misery is in fact Kim Jong Il and his regime.

North Korean defectors are sending remittances to their families, helping demonstrate the prosperity in South Korea. North Korea now has a cell phone system with well over 500,000 subscribers. And although you cannot call directly from South Korea, defectors pay brokers in China to contact their families.

We also see the defectors themselves getting information into North Korea from DVDs, VCDs, USBs and flash drives through China and other creative means such as balloon launches. North Koreans, especially the elites, are keeping up with South Korean soap operas and watching many South Korean, as well, as western films. Therefore, it is more important than ever to raise the human rights concerns so that they know our concerns are for them.

For example, it was a brilliant action by the Obama administration to include Special Envoy for North Korea Human Rights Ambassador King in the delegation that went to North Korea to assess the food situation. This underscored the fact that it is the human rights conditions in North Korea that are causing the starvation. Furthermore, North Koreans are no longer dependent on Kim Jong Il's regime to survive, as over 200 private markets are functioning and the regime has given up trying to control them. This capitalism is saving them from experiencing the same level of starvation that led to the deaths of millions during the famine.

Kim Jong Il's unprovoked attacks on South Korea, as Congressman Payne just mentioned, have awakened South Koreans to the truth that we must not ignore the human rights of North Koreans for the false promise of this regime to end its nuclear program.

To take advantage of these changes, governments, nongovernmental organizations, and individuals first of all should make human rights central to all negotiations with or about North Korea.

Second, we should only provide food when relief organizations can stay and monitor it to the point of consumption; otherwise it will most assuredly be diverted to maintain the regime that is causing the starvation in the first place.

Third, we need to continue to support radio broadcasting, especially programs like Radio Free Asia and Voice of America and the independent radio broadcasters like Free North Korea Radio, a defector-led station in Seoul.

Fourth, we need to empower the defector organizations that are using creative methods to get information into North Korea, like Fighters for a Free North Korea and the North Korea People's Liberation Front.

Five, we must convince the Chinese to end their brutal policy of forced repatriation for North Korean refugees, which is prolonging this crisis by giving Kim Jong Il a reason to resist any reforms that would improve the situation in that country so that North Koreans do not want to risk their lives trying to flee.

Six, we should support the 12 North Korean defector churches. For example, I have been working to try to connect churches here in the United States with these defector churches that have been formed in South Korea.

Seven, we need to put the elites in this regime on notice that they will be held accountable for their crimes against the North Korean people.

Last week, a North Korean assassin was caught. His mission was to kill Park Sang Hak who heads Fires for a Free North Korea. Park Sang Hak is the one that has been doing the balloon launches sending in information. Both Park and Kim Seung Min, who leads Free North Korea Radio, who is here at this hearing, have been regularly targeted by assassins sent by Kim Jong Il. What this tells us is that what they are doing is the most effective work.

At the end of 2009, Free North Korea Radio started broadcasting Voices from the People. These were actual interviews from inside the country that they broadcast back in. Supporting this flow of information through radio broadcasting, especially by North Korean defectors, is the most effective way to reach the people because the Internet is only available to the elites in the regime.

Recently, the North Korea People's Liberation Front was formed by former North Korean military, including officers, special forces, cyber warfare experts, and propaganda specialists. This is significant because the only time there was organized opposition against the regime was from the military who had studied in the Soviet Union and came back to North Korea wanting reform. Although they were eventually discovered, they operated against the regime from 1989 until 1994. Because all North Korean males must serve for 10 years and the elites are exempt from service, this means that the North Korean military truly represents the people.

We saw the Army in Romania turn against Kim Il Sung and Kim Jong Il's good friend Nicholae Ceausescu when the people of that country rose up against their dictator. Right now, the elites in power have absolutely no incentive to oppose Kim Jong Il because their entire lives are based on the successful transfer of power to Kim Jong Un. We must assure them that they would have a stake in the future if North Korea opens up to reform.

Because North Koreans are citizens under South Korea, under the Korean Constitution, South Korea has an important role to play, and they should convene a tribunal of respected judges to begin the prosecution of those in the regime responsible for the political prison camps and these other atrocities.

There are 23,000 eyewitnesses now, and we should start naming the names of those who are committing these crimes. When North Korea finally opens up, I believe we will be even more horrified at the atrocities that the Kim regimes have committed against the North Korean people that today are beyond our imagination. We will face the same questions that the world faced when the allies liberated the Nazi death camps: What did you know and what did you do to help stop our tragic circumstances?

Thank you, Mr. Chairman.

Mr. SMITH. Ms. Scholte, thank you very much for your testimony and for your leadership all these years, and for that very incisive testimony.

[The prepared statement of Ms. Suzanne Scholte follows:]

Suzanne Scholte
President, Defense Forum Foundation
September 20, 2011
House Committee on Foreign Affairs, Subcommittee on Africa, Global Health, and Human Rights

It is an honor to testify before this Subcommittee which is chaired by two men I greatly admire. I have had the great honor of working with both Congressman Chris Smith and Donald Payne not only on North Korea but also on a number of other issues including our shared desire to see the Sahrawi people of Western Sahara finally achieve self-determination.

In today's testimony I want to make two main points the first is that North Korea continues to be one of the darkest places on Earth, and we have failed to address the main issue of North Korea which is human rights because we have focused instead on the nuclear issue. This has had tragic results.

Secondly, despite the ongoing human rights tragedy in North Korea, there is great hope because things have changed dramatically in that country. But if we fail to enact the policies that address the human rights conditions and fail to empower those who can advocate for peaceful change in North Korea, then we will most certainly end up prolonging this deadly regime.

While we witness people rising up in repressive societies most recently in North Africa and the Middle East, we wonder why do the North Koreans, who are arguably the most persecuted people in the world, not rise up? It is precisely because they are the most persecuted in the world. In fact, North Koreans are the only people in the world that do not enjoy one single human right that is enshrined in the Universal Declaration of Human Rights a document adopted in 1948, the same year that Kim II Sung came to power.

This Declaration was in response to the atrocities committed by the Axis powers during World War II. When the Nazi death camps were liberated by the Allied forces during that war, the international community vowed NEVER AGAIN would we allow these kinds of atrocities to occur.

Yet, today, the political prison camps in North Korea have existed longer than the Soviet gulag the Chinese Laogai or the Nazi death camps. In preparation for regime succession, it is feared that they will expand in numbers as Amnesty International has reported recently.

Your two defector witnesses today are living proof of the horrors of these camps as well as the length of their existence -- one was imprisoned in Yoduk in the 1970s while another was imprisoned for 28 years up through the beginning of this decade in Bukchang.

In addition to political prison camps, we have seen millions of North Koreans starve to death despite billions of food aid and economic assistance. North Koreans are not the only ones who suffer from Kim Jong-il's brutal dictatorship but South Korean POWs are still being held in North Korea, while at least 180,308 captives are being held against their will in North Korea including 80,000 abductees from South Korea and hundreds of others from thirteen countries as recently documented by the Committee for Human Rights in North Korea.

The policy of our government in the past has been to sideline these human rights concerns with the hope of engaging North Korea to give up their nuclear ambitions. For example, former Presidents Bill Clinton and George Bush set out with the best intentions to engage North Korea to give up their nuclear ambitions through Clinton's Agreed Framework and through Bush's Six Party Talks. Both helped provide food aid to North Korea to try to stop the deaths of millions from starvation. Both intentionally sidelined human rights concerns, making them secondary to addressing North Korea's nuclear ambitions.

Despite their efforts, North Korea's nuclear ambitions were never thwarted, their proliferation of their nuclear technology to countries including Iran and Syria continues, and North Korea declared it would never give up its nuclear weapons. Any of the defectors could tell you that Kim Jong-il would never give up his nuclear weapons. He may be an evil dictator but he has brilliantly manipulated the good intentions of both America and South Korea.

My second main point is that there is great hope because things are increasingly changing in that country. Despite Kim Jong-il's best efforts to literally keep North Koreans "in the dark" and isolated from the rest of the world, up to 60 percent of North Koreans have access to some form of information beyond the regime's propaganda. They are no longer isolated and are increasingly learning the reality that the source of their misery is not America or South Korea, but the source of their misery is Kim Jong il and the elites of his regime. North Korean defectors are sending remittances to their families in North Korea, helping them to survive which also demonstrates the prosperity in South Korea. North Korea now has a cell phone system with 500,000 subscribers according to Orascom Telecom and although you cannot call from South Korea, defectors are paying brokers in China to contact their families in North Korea. We also see the defectors getting information into North Korea from DVDs, VCDs, and USBs through China and other creative means such as balloon launches. In fact, North Koreans are keeping up with South Korean soap operas and watching many South Korean as well as Western films especially the elites.

Because North Koreans are getting more information from the outside world, it is more important than ever before to raise these human rights concerns so that they know our concerns are for them. For example, it was brilliant action by the Obama administration to include the Special Envoy for North Korean Human Rights Ambassador Robert King in the delegation that went to North Korea to assess the food situation. This underscored the fact that it is the human rights conditions in North Korea that are causing the starvation in the first place, because of the diversion of aid by the Kim Jong-il regime and his failed policies.

Furthermore, North Koreans are no longer dependent on Kim Jong-il's regime to survive as over 200 private markets are functioning in North Korea and the regime has given up trying to control these markets. Capitalism is saving the North Koreans from experiencing the level of starvation that led to the deaths of millions of innocent men, women and children during the recent famine.

Perhaps, most significantly, Kim Jong-il's unprovoked and brutal attacks on South Korea have awakened South Koreans, as well as former Bush administration officials, to the truth that we must not ignore the human rights of North Koreans for the false promises of this regime to end its nuclear program. Furthermore, South Korean young people are taking up this cause which was so critical to the democratization of the Republic of Korea.

However, despite these amazing changes, North Koreans are still the most suffering people on earth. Nowhere else on Earth can someone be shot for making a long distance phone call or visiting another country, nowhere else on Earth can a child be born and spend their life in a political prison camp. Nowhere else on Earth have millions died in a famine in a so called "industrialized nation" during peacetime. No so called "government" on Earth except North Korea sanctions the abduction of citizens from other nations, holds Korean War POWs, counterfeits money, and trafficks in drugs.

To take advantage of the changes inside the country, the free world including governments, non- governmental organizations and individuals should:
1) make human rights central to all negotiations with or about North Korea;
2) only provide food when relief organizations can stay and monitor it to the point of consumption otherwise it will most assuredly be diverted to maintain the regime that is causing the starvation in the first place;
3) continue to support radio broadcasting especially programs like Radio Free Asia and the independent radio broadcasters like Free North Korea Radio, a defector led station in Seoul;
4) empower the defector organizations that are using creative methods to get information into North Korea like Fighters for a Free North Korea and the North Korea People's Liberation Front;
5) convince China to end their brutal policy of forced repatriation for North Korean refugees which is prolonging this crisis by giving Kim Jong-il a reason to resist any reforms that would improve the situation in the country so that North Koreans do not want to risk their lives to flee
6) support the twelve North Korean defector churches – for example, I have been working

to try to connect churches here in the U.S. with these defector churches that have formed in South Korea. These North Korean defector churches, like their South Korean counterparts, are very missions oriented and their number one mission is North Korea. They are not afraid to speak truth into the darkness in that country.
7) put the "elites" in this regime on notice that they will be held accountable for their crimes against the North Korean people

We are at a pivotal moment in the history of the Korean peninsula because we are at a cross roads on which way will we choose to move forward? The appeasement of the past that led to millions of deaths or working with the 23,000 North Korean defectors that have successfully fled that country.

One of the most important actions we can take is to empower the North Korean defectors to carry out their work for peaceful change and reunification. Last week, a North Korean assassin was caught – his mission was to kill Park Sang Hak who leads Fighters for a Free North Korea. Both Park and Kim Seung Min, who leads Free North Korea Radio and is at this hearing have been regularly targeted by assassins sent by the Kim Jong-il regime.

What does that tell us? That they are doing the most effective work.

We see signs of increasing discontent inside North Korea similar to the signs in the late totalitarian regimes in Eastern Europe. For example, the regime attempted through several means to shut down the private markets but had to back off because of open opposition. We saw at the end of 2009 amazing breakthroughs in information gathering. Free North Korea Radio had started broadcasting Voices from the People – actually interviews recorded from inside the country that they broadcast back in – a significant achievement as these defectors and their network are an important act of resistance in themselves.

Supporting this free flow of information though radio broadcasting especially by North Korean defectors is the most effective way to reach the North Korean people because the internet is only available to a small regime elite.

Furthermore, there is another defector organization. The North Korean People's Liberation Front which was established last fall. It was formed by former North Korean military, both officers and enlisted soldiers including special forces, cyberwarfare experts, propaganda specialists. This is significant because the only time there was organized opposition against the regime was from the military. Military leaders who had studied in the Soviet Union returned to North Korea with the desire for the country to open up to reform. They operated against the regime from 1989 until 1994. Although they were eventually discovered, and most of them executed, they were able to operate for at least 5 years.

Two significant aspects about the North Korean military; all North Korean males must serve for ten years and the elites are exempt. This means that the North Korean military truly represents the North Korean people.

Remember what happened to Kim Il Sung and Kim Jong il's good friend, Nicolae Ceausescu in Romania. The army turned against this dictator in favor of the people. We saw this happen recently in Egypt.

Just as the North Korean people are realizing that the source of their misery is Kim Jong-il, the North Korean military must also realize their enemy is regime of Kim Jong-il as this regime has killed more North Koreans than were killed during the Korean War.

Furthermore, we must put the "elites" on notice that we will stand with them but only if they oppose this regime. Right now they have absolutely no incentive to oppose Kim Jong il because their entire lives are based on the successful transfer of power to Kim Jong Eun. We must assure them that they would have a stake in the future if North Korean opens up to reform. The elites that have defected know and understand this.

Also, I have been recommending that South Korea convene a tribunal of respected judges to begin the prosecution of those in the regime responsible for the political prison camps, the attacks on South Korea, the misappropriation of food aid and other atrocities.

Because North Koreans are citizens of South Korea under the Korean constitution, they have legal standing in South Korea. There are 23,000 eyewitnesses and defector groups like Free the NK Gulag and South Korean NGOS like the Database Center for North Korea Human Rights and the Korean Institute for National Unification have all the evidence that is needed. Start naming names now and print their names along with their photos or sketches of their faces so that the public will see the faces of those who are committing these atrocities.

It is inevitable that Kim Jong-il's regime will end. It is inevitable that North Korea will open up. And when North Korea opens up, we will be even more horrified and shocked at the atrocities that Kim Il Song and Kim Jong-il have committed against the North Korean people that today are beyond our imagination. We will face the same questions that the world faced when the Allies liberated the Nazi death camps: What did you know and what did you do to help stop our tragic circumstances? The time to act is NOW, so that when unification comes, we can proudly answer that question.

##

Mr. SMITH. We will now hear from Ms. Kim Young Soon.

STATEMENT OF MS. KIM YOUNG SOON, VICE PRESIDENT, COMMITTEE FOR THE DEMOCRATIZATION OF NORTH KOREA

Ms. KIM YOUNG SOON. Hello. My name is Kim Young Soon, author of I was a Friend of Sung Hae Rim. I am a North Korean defector and a survivor of North Korean political prison camp, Yoduk, camp number 15. First of all, I want to thank the Members of the United States Congress and related officials of the Congress for giving me a chance to speak at this important venue. I also would like to thank Ms. Suzanne Scholte of the Defense Forum Foundation for her years of friendship and for listening to my story of the North Korean political prison camp experience.

Camp number 15 Yoduk where I was incarcerated is now well known throughout the world. Yoduk political prison camp was created in July 1969 under orders of Kim Il Sung in Yoduk-gun in South Hamkyung Province in a region known for its rough and mountainous features. It is here that for 30 years people who have incurred the wrath of Kim Il Sung and Kim Jong Il have been sent for the crime of being a political prisoner and where they have died silent deaths.

I wrote of my time at Yoduk into a book entitled I Was a Friend of Sung Hae Rim. Sung Hae Rim was at one point in my life my friend and also the hidden mistress of Kim Jong Il, and anyone who knew the secret in North Korea were either executed or sent to political prison camps. I became a victim of this myself and was therefore sent to Yoduk. I want to tell the world about what happened to me and also tell the world about the reality of the North Korean political prison camp system.

The Worker's Party's establishment of the One Thought Principle was instituted whereby the citizens were sent to prison camps for total isolation from the general public—general society for the following crimes: The crime of defaming the authority and prestige of Kim Il Sung and Kim Jong Il; the crime of knowledge about the private life of Kim Jong Il and leaking information about it to the general public, thus defaming the prestige of the great leader.

When I was sent to the prison camp I had no knowledge about these facts. The following are the political crimes that I came to know of after I was incarcerated in the Yoduk prison camp: The crime of talking about the cyst or lump on Kim Il Sung's neck; or the crime of unwittingly damaging or soiling the statue or portrait of Kim Il Sung; the crime of knowing about the private life of Kim Jong Il, for example, knowing about Sung Hae Rim being the secret mistress of Kim Jong Il and disclosing this information to an outsider; the crime of revealing the birth of Kim Jong Nam, the firstborn son of Kim Jong Il; the crime of listening to or viewing foreign radio or TV broadcast; the crime of questioning or criticizing the policy of the Worker's Party; and the crime of expressing criticism or complaints about North Korean society.

I was a close friend—I was close friends with Sung Hae Rim, having gone to the same school with her from girl's high school to college, and one day I heard directly from her that she will be going to Special Residence number five. At that time, those in the know knew that Special Residence number five meant the residence of Kim Il Sung and Kim Jong Il. However, at the time I was taken to the political prison camp, I had no idea why I was being incarcerated. And it was only in the summer of 1989, after I was released, did I find out the reason why from a state security agent in Pyongyang.

The security agent said the following to me: "Sung Hae Rim was not the wife of Kim Jong Il nor did she bear him a son. These are all groundless rumors. If you mention anything about this again you will not be forgiven."

I would like to talk briefly about my interrogation before I was sent to the political prison camp. On August 1, 1970, I was forced into a car by state security agents and taken to a secret location where I was interrogated for 2 months by a unit called Unit 312 for preliminary investigation in a state security investigation room. Under extreme fear for 2 months, I was told to write my entire life story and to include everything and leave out nothing, so I wrote on and on.

In my writing I confessed and wrote about Sung Hae Rim coming over to my house and telling me that she would be going to Special Residence number five, and also admitted that people around me knew this information as well. After the investigations were over on October 1, 1970, my entire family and I, seven people in total, were sent to Yoduk political prison camp. The person who committed the crime was labeled the conspirator or ring leader, while those taken along for yeon-jwa-jweh, a Korean word for guilt by association, were labeled nonprincipal criminals, and this was how the criminals in the prison camp were classified. We woke up at 3:30 in the morning to go to work by 4:30 a.m. And the labor was from sun-up until sun-down. Meals had to be provided by ourselves through self-sufficiency. I saw countless prisoners contract the disease pellagra and suffer from diarrhea and die.

After work was finished there were daily Fight for Ideology meetings for all the prisoners. Those who were unfortunate enough to be caught by security agents during these ideology meetings and sent away in shackles were never seen again.

The forced manual labor was beyond anyone's imagination, and in case of falling short of work goals, the whole group was punished. There were so many dead bodies that I saw there, enough to fill up a field. My three sons, one daughter, father and mother, died from starvation. There were no coffins so their bodies were rolled in a straw mat and buried. One of my sons, who was 9 years old at the time, drowned to death in Ryongyung River which is near the prison camp. My daughter was given away for adoption after our release so that she can have a better life. To this day I do not know about her whereabouts, whether she is alive or dead. My youngest son was publicly executed by a firing squad for trying to escape North Korea after his release and attempting to go to South Korea in 1993 at the age of 23. My husband was sent to another political prison camp, a total and complete control zone, on July 4, 1970, and to this day I do not know whether he is dead or alive.

So from my original family of eight people, currently only two have survived and successfully escaped from North Korea—myself and another son. The rest of my family, six people, have all died.

My older brother, who was the pillar of our family, was a colonel in the North Korean Army during the North Korea War, serving the North Korean 3rd Infantry, and while on a mission for the division commander, he was killed in battle at the age of 25. Accordingly, our family received favors for my brother's heroic acts from Kim Il Sung and we lived well until our family was sent to a political prison camp. And as a result of feeling betrayed, I escaped from North Korea. Even after I was released from Yoduk political prison camp, I was classified as an anti-regime reactionary and suffered under the monitoring by the state security apparatus. I escaped North Korea on February 1, 2001, and entered South Korea in November 2003.

In conclusion, I would just like to say that in the political prison camps in North Korea, it is a place where the prisoners will eat anything that flies, crawls, or grows in the field. I wasted 9 years of the prime of my life in that hellhole of a place where even animals turn their faces away. I lost all my family members and have lived a life of tears, of blood, and extreme hardship.

Please save the 23 million people in North Korea who are living a life of misery not unlike what I had suffered. Even though I am now over 70 years old, I will fight for the freedom of my people, my countrymen, until all my strength is expended. This is the reason why I have lived so far and I believe also my purpose.

On that note I want to deeply thank, again, the members of this committee for your interest in the human rights situation of North Korea, especially the political prison camps. Thank you.

Mr. SMITH. Ms. Kim, thank you so much. The brutality that you yourself have suffered and the loss of your family members, including a daughter who, as you said was adopted obviously without your permission, you have no idea where she is, your husband you have no idea where he is and the loss of your other family members, just underscores the brutality of Kim Jong Il; and the fact that the West, the United States and any country that has any sense of compassion, needs to speak out against this horrific abuse. And this should not be a second-tier issue, the human rights abuses that are commonplace in North Korea. So we thank you for making us further aware of the extreme barbarity you have been made to endure and your family.

[The prepared statement of Ms. Kim Young Soon follows:]

Young Soon KIM
Vice President, Committee for the Democratization of North Korea
September 20, 2011
House Committee on Foreign Affairs Subcommittee on Africa, Global Health and
Human Rights

Hello, my name is KIM, Young Soon, author of 'I Was a Friend of Sung Hae Rim'. I
am a North Korean defector and a survivor of the North Korean political prison
camp, Yoduk (camp #15).

First of all, I want to thank the Members of the United States Congress and related
officials of the Congress for giving me a chance to speak at this important venue. I
also would like to thank Ms. Suzanne Scholte of the Defense Forum Foundation for
her years of friendship and for listening to my story of the North Korean political
prison camp.

Camp number 15, Yoduk, where I was incarcerated, is now well known throughout
the world. Yoduk Prison Camp was created in July of 1969 under orders of Kim Il
Sung, in Yoduk-gun, South Hamkyung Province, in a region known for its rough
and mountainous features. It is here that for 30 years people who have incurred
the wrath of Kim Il Sung and Kim Jong-il have been sent for the 'crime' of being a
political prisoner and died silent deaths.

I wrote of my time at Yoduk into a book and titled it 'I Was a Friend of Sung Hae
Rim'. Sung Hae Rim was at one point in my life my friend and also a hidden
mistress of Kim Jong-il, and anyone who knew this secret in North Korea were
either executed or sent to political prison camps, and I became a victim of this
myself and was sent to Yoduk; I want to tell the world about what happened to me
and also tell the world about the reality of the North Korean political prison camp
system.

Why I was sent to Camp Number 15 (Political Prison Camp)

The Worker's Party's establishment of the 'One Thought Principle' was instituted
whereby the citizens were sent to prison camps for total isolation from general
society for the following crimes: the crime of defaming the authority and prestige of
Kim Il Sung and Kim Jong-il; the crime of knowledge about the private life of Kim
Jong-il and leaking information about it to the general public, thus defaming the
prestige of the Great Leader. When I was sent to the prison camp, I had no
knowledge about these facts.

**Other political crimes that I came to know of after I was incarcerated in the
prison camp.**

"The crime of talking about a cyst/lump on Kim Il Sung's neck."

"The crime of (unwittingly) damaging or soiling the statue or portrait of Kim Il Sung."

"The crime of knowing about the private life of Kim Jong-il. For example, knowing about Sung Hae Rim being the hidden mistress of Kim Jong-il, and disclosing this information to an outsider."

"The crime of revealing the birth of Kim Jong Nam, the firstborn son of Kim Jong-il"

"The crime of listening to or viewing foreign radio or TV."

"The crime of questioning or criticizing the policy of the Worker's Party."

"The crime of expressing criticism or complaints about North Korea society."

I was close friends with Sung Hae Rim, having gone to the same school with her from girl's high school to college, and one day I heard directly from her that she would be 'going to the Special Residence #5'; at that time, those in the know knew that 'Special Residence #5' meant the residence of Kim Il Sung and Kim Jong-il.

However, at the time I was taken to the political prison camp, I had no idea why I was being incarcerated, and it was only in the summer of 1989 after I was released did I find out the reason why, from a state security agent in Pyongyang. The security agent said the following to me: "Sung Hae Rim was not the wife of Kim Jong-il nor did she bear him a son. These are all groundless rumors. If you mention anything about this again you will not be forgiven."

Interrogation and life in the political prison camp

On August 1st, 1970, I was forced into a car by state security agents and taken to a secret location where I was interrogated for two months by Unit 312 for preliminary investigation in a state security interrogation room. Under extreme fear for two months, I was told to write my entire life story, and include everything and leave out nothing, and I wrote on and on. IN my writing, I confessed and wrote about Sung Hae Rim coming over to my house and telling me that she would be going to Special Residence #5, and also admitted that people around me knew this information as well.

After the investigations were over, on October 1st, 1970, my entire family and I (7 people total) were sent to Yoduk Political Prison Camp.

- The person who committed the crime was labeled the 'conspirator/ringleader' while those taken along for 'yeon-jwa-jweh' (guilt by association) were labeled 'non-principal criminal' – this was how the criminals were classified.
- We woke up at 3:30 in the morning to go to work by 4:30am, and the labor was from sun up until sun down.
- Meals had to be provided by ourselves, through self-sufficiency.
- I saw countless prisoners contract pellagra, and suffer from diarrhea and die.
- After work was finished, there were daily 'Fight for Ideology' meetings.

- Those who were unfortunate enough to be caught by security agents during the ideology meetings and sent away in shackles, were never seen again.
- The forced manual labor was beyond anyone's imagination, and in case of falling short of work goals, the whole group was punished.
- There were so many dead bodies, enough to fill up a field.
- My three sons, one daughter, father and mother, died from starvation; there were no coffins so their bodies were rolled in a straw mat and buried.
- One of my sons, who was 9 years old at the time, drowned to death in Ryongyung River, which is near the prison camp.
- My daughter was given away for adoption, after our release; to this day, I do not know about her whereabouts, whether she is alive or dead.
- My youngest son was publicly executed by firing squad for trying to escape North Korea after his release and attempting to go to South Korea, in 1993 at the age of 23.
- My husband was sent to another political prison camp, a total and complete control zone, in July 4th, 1970, and to this day I do not know whether he is dead or alive.
- From our original family of 8 people, currently only two have survived and successfully escaped from North Korea (myself and another son), the rest of my family, 6 people, have all died.

My older brother, who was the pillar of our family, was a colonel in the North Korean army during the Korean War, in the 3rd Infantry, and while on a mission for the division commander, was killed in battle at the age of 25. Accordingly, our family received favors from Kim Il Sung and lived well until being sent to a political prison camp, and as a result of feeling betrayed, I escaped from North Korea. Even after I was released from Yoduk political prison camp, I was classified as an anti-regime reactionary and suffered under the monitoring by the state security apparatus.

I escaped North Korea on February 1st, 2001, and entered South Korea in November of 2003.

In Conclusion
In the political prison camps of North Korea is a place where the political prisoners will eat anything that 'flies, crawls, grows in the field'.

I wasted 9 years of the prime of my life in that hellhole of a place where even animals will turn their faces away; I lost all my family members, and have lived a life of tears of blood and extreme hardship. Please save the 23 million people in North Korea who are living a life of misery not unlike what I suffered.

Even though I am now over 70 years old, I will fight for the freedom of my people, my countrymen until all my strength is expended. This is the reason why I have lived so far, and also my purpose. In that note I want to deeply thank again the members of the United States Congress for your interest in the human rights situation of North Korea, especially the political prison camps.

Thank you.

Mr. SMITH. We will now hear from another Ms. Kim who has suffered three decades in the gulag and we look forward to hearing her testimony.

STATEMENT OF MS. KIM HYE SOOK, LONGEST-SERVING SURVIVOR OF NORTH KOREAN PRISON CAMPS

Ms. KIM HYE SOOK [through interpreter]. Hello, my name is Kim Hye Sook. I am a North Korean defector who was incarcerated in political prison camp number 18, Bukchang prison camp, in Bukchang-gun South Pyongang Province for 28 years, and in 2009 I escaped North Korea and entered South Korea via China, Laos, and Thailand.

In February 1975 for reasons that were unknown to me at that time, I was dragged with my parents to the prison camp. I was 13 years old at the time. During my incarceration at camp number 18 I lost my grandmother, mother, brother and my husband. I only found out after I was out of that hell-on-earth camp number 18 why I was sent to the prison camp: Because my grandfather had defected South Korea during the Korean War. But by then I had nowhere to go and complain about this situation.

I would like to say that the term "kwan-li-so" in North Korea is a living hell for human beings, a place where people who have committed so-called crimes are sent and incarcerated as a group and forced to work in manual slave labor. There are political prison camps where people who have been found guilty of being against Kim Il Sung and Kim Jong Il or those resisting the regime are sent and held; whereas in places like camp number 18 where I was incarcerated in, besides political prisoners, those who are guilty of economic crimes are sent along with family members and are forced to work in coal mines.

In camp number 18 in Bukchang where I was imprisoned, the whole prison camp was encircled by high electrified fence, and trying to escape through this over 3,000 volts of electrified fence was unimaginable.

When I first entered the prison camp we were told to memorize ten rules of the prison camp. And I remember it vividly because I remembered them from such an early age. One of the rules was that the prisoners were not supposed to know the reason for ending up in the prison camp, and those found violating this rule will be relentlessly executed by a firing squad. For young people like me, who ended up in the prison camp at a young age, we were given very rudimentary education, basic Korean language education, and then when we turned 16 or 17, everyone without exception was sent to the coal mines to dig out coal, and this goes without saying for the adults as well.

We had to work 16–18 hour work days without rest or holidays. And for food, our family of seven was provided only around ten pounds of corn per month. And this was supplemented by gruel made from grass or anything that we picked from the field, tree bark, grass, and that is what we ate, one meal a day, corn and the mixed grass gruel that we had to make for ourselves.

Mr. SMITH. Ms. Kim, if you could just suspend for one brief moment. We are joined by the chairman of the Appropriations Subcommittee that deals with justice issues and science, but is also the author of the International Religious Freedom Act of 1998. As we all know, North Korea is a Tier III trafficking country. It is Congressman Frank Wolf who cares deeply about human rights, but he can only stay a brief minute.

Mr. WOLF. Thank you, Mr. Smith. I want to thank you and Mr. Payne and the committee for having this hearing. I met with the witnesses earlier today. It was one of the most significant and moving testimony and reports that I have ever ever heard. And I think certainly the State Department should do everything they can, quite frankly, to bring about regime change in North Korea.

When this government falls, as it will fall, the same way the East German Government fell with regard to the Berlin Wall, the West will feel so guilty to know that it said nothing, other than the hearings that the members here have had, has said nothing with regard to what takes place. This administration should do everything.

And lastly, and I will end with this. I think the church in the West, all religious faiths in the West, should come together and support these people in every way they can, to see about that the fact that hundreds of thousands are in these camps is totally unacceptable. So anyone within the Voice who can hear this, can follow this hearing. Ought to be advocating it.

So I want to again thank you, Mr. Payne, and the other members, and thank the witnesses for coming by my office. I am on my way to a 4 o'clock, but I was just moved to come by because what I heard was just so powerful. And with that, Mr. Chairman, I yield back. I thank you very much.

Mr. SMITH. Chairman Wolf, thank you very much. Ms. Kim, if you could continue.

Ms. KIM HYE SOOK. And I was plagued with hunger from the day I entered the prison camp until the day I was released. And my one wish was to just eat one bowl of white rice for one meal. After I became an adult and during my times of working at the coal mine, walking to and from work, I would look around for anything to eat. And regardless of season, it became a habit to scrape or pluck anything that was green and make soup and eat it, whether it was from tree bark or from grass. I cannot even begin to describe how many people suffered and died because of starvation in the prison camp and how many people were killed without reason for not listening to authorities or not showing enough repentance. Though public execution by firing squad—through public execution by firing squad, their bodies were riddled with countless bullet holes, and I saw countless bodies that ended up like this. There was a time when I saw the bodies of people who were killed by firing squad were rolled up in a straw mat and carried away in carts, and I said to myself even dogs will not die so pitifully.

In this place where human lives were worthless than those of flies, this was where my brother and husband died also. Their deaths were classified as due to accidents, but their deaths were intentional deaths carried out in the atmosphere of the prison camps where nothing was normal.

And as a result of working the coal mines for over 12 years, I contracted black lung and faced death many times. But in place of my mother, who passed away before me, I vow to survive and live on and look after my siblings, my remaining siblings, and that devotion was what allowed me to survive that hell. And my siblings are still incarcerated at camp number 18, my brother and sister.

And in December 1974, before our family was sent off to prison camp, camp number 18, my father was hauled away by the State Security Bureau, never to be heard from again. I do not know what happened to him to this day. And even at this moment as I speak, there are over 10,000 people—20,000 people who are in camp 18 without knowing the reason why, people who are dying from abuse and lack of rights at this very moment.

And this is not just happening in camp number 18, but I would like to say that this is the suffering and sadness that 23 million North Korean citizens are going through and suffering, experiencing right now.

Not only that, but besides the human rights violations going on in North Korea, there is now the cruelty and misery inflicted on North Korean refugee women who have escaped North Korea into China through the terrible situation of human trafficking happening in different places. After narrowly escaping death and coming out of North Korea and into China and then becoming victims of human and sexual trafficking, I can say with authority that the tragic situation of the North Korean refugee women must be told again and again in the international community. I myself was sold four different times in four different cities in China. And the inhumane and the indescribable suffering that these women go through in China, being sold like commodity, still keeps me awake at night.

Please end the existence of such a society and make it into a place where humans can live as people. Please let the people without any rights in North Korea live in freedom and happiness. Please get rid of the political prison camps, and please tell those who do not know about freedom what freedom is about.

I sincerely hope that my earnest pleas will be delivered to the United States Congress, to the United States Government, and to the people of America. I also want to deeply thank the honorable members of this committee here today who have made it possible for me to speak, as well as Ms. Suzanne Scholte of the Defense Forum Foundation.

Thank you.

[The prepared statement of Kim Hye Sook follows:]

Hye Sook KIM
Member , Free the NK Gulag
September 20, 2011
House Committee on Foreign Affairs Subcommittee on Africa, Global Health and
Human Rights

Hello, my name is Kim Hye Sook.

I am a North Korean defector who was incarcerated in political prison camp
number 18, Bukchang prison camp, in Bukchang-gun, South Pyongang Province,
for 28 years, and in 2009 I escaped North Korea and entered South Korea via
China, Laos, and Thailand.

In February of 1975, for reasons that were unknown to me at the time, I was
dragged with my parents to the prison camp. I was 13 years old the time. During
my incarceration at camp number 18, I lost my grandmother, mother, brother, and
my husband.

I only found out after I was out of that that hell on earth, camp number 18, why I
was sent to the prison camp – because my grandfather had defected to South
Korea during the Korean War, but by then I had nowhere to go to complain about
this.

I would like to say that the term 'kwan-li-so' in North Korea is a living hell for human
beings, a place where people who have committed so-called crimes are sent and
incarcerated as a group, and forced to work in manual slave labor.

There are political prison camps where people who have been found guilty of being
against Kim Il Sung and Kim Jong-il or those resisting the regime are sent and held,
whereas in places like camp number 18 where I was incarcerated in, besides
political prisoners those who are guilty of economic crimes are sent along with
family members and are forced to work in coal mines.

In camp number 18 in Bukchang where I was imprisoned, the whole prison camp
was encircled by 13-foot high electrified fence, and trying to escape through this
3,300 volt electrified fence was unimaginable.

When I first entered the prison camp, we were told to memorize 10 articles/rules of
the prison camp, and I still remember it vividly because I remembered them from
such an early age. One of the rules was that prisoners were not supposed to know
the reason for ending up in the prison camp, and those caught violating this rule
will be relentlessly executed by a firing squad.

For young people like me who ended up in the prison camp at a young age, we were given very rudimentary education, and then when we turned 16 or 17, everyone without exception was sent to the coalmines to dig out coal – this goes without saying for the adults as well.

We had to work 16 to 18 hour work days without rest or holidays, and for food, our family of seven was provided only around 10 pounds of corn per month.

I was plagued with hunger from the day I entered the prison camp and until the day I was released. My one wish was to eat just one bowl of white rice for one meal. After I became an adult and during my times of working at the coalmine and walking to and from work, I would look around for anything to eat, and regardless of season it became a habit to scrape or pluck anything that was green and make soup and eat it.

I cannot even begin to describe how many people suffered and died because of starvation in the prison camp, and how many people were killed without reason for not listening to authorities or not showing enough 'repentance', though public executions by firing squad, their bodies riddled with countless bullet holes.

There was a time when I saw the bodies of people who were killed by firing squad who were rolled up in straw mats and carried away in carts, and said to myself, 'even dogs will not die so pitifully'.

In this place where human lives were worth less than those of flies, was where my brother and husband died also. Their deaths were classified as due to accidents, but their deaths were intentional deaths carried out in the atmosphere of the prison camp where there was nothing normal. As a result, I also lost my grandmother, father and mother, and my brother, all of who were sent to camp number 18 with me.

As a result of working in the coalmines I contracted Pneumoconiosis ('black lung'), and faced death many times, but in place of my mother who passed away before me, I vowed to survive and live on and look out after my remaining siblings, and that devotion was what allowed me to survive that hell.

My siblings are still incarcerated at camp number 18. In December of 1974, before our family was sent off to camp number 18, my father was hauled away by the state security bureau, never to be heard from again. I do not know what happened to him, to this day. And even at this moment, there are over 10,000 people who are in camp 18 without knowing the reason why, people who are dying from abuse and lack or rights...

And this is not just happening in camp number 18, but I would like to say that this is the suffering and sadness that 23 millions North Korean citizens are going through and experiencing.

Not only that, but besides the human rights violations going on in North Korea, there is now cruelty and misery inflicted on North Korean refugee women who have escaped North Korea into China, through the terrible situation of human trafficking happening in different places.

After narrowly escaping death and coming out of North Korea and into China and third countries, and then becoming victims of human and sexual trafficking, I can say with authority that the tragic situation of the North Korean refugee women must be told and told again in the international community.

North Korea is a country where in the 21st century, political prison camps are in existence and a society where in the prison camps the lives of human beings are more easily disposed of than those of animals. A society where the whole country is a prison. A society where those who escaped the country in search of freedom are caught and imprisoned and executed, and where those who have escaped become lost people and orphans in the international community. A society where chastity and virginity, which is more precious than life, is sold cheaper than the cheapest of things...

Please end the existence of such a society, and make it into a place where humans can live as people. Please let the people without any rights in North Korea live in freedom and happiness, please get rid of the political prison camps, and please tell those who do not know about freedom, what freedom is about!

I sincerely hope that my earnest pleas will be delivered to the United States Congress, to the United States Government, and to the people of America. I also want to deeply thank the honorable Members of Congress here today who have made it possible for me to speak, as well as to Ms. Suzanne Scholte of the Defense Forum Foundation.

I am encouraged that through my presence here today, by exposing the inhumane atrocities happening in the North Korean political prison camps, the crimes against humanity perpetrated by the North Korean regime can be condemned. I believe that one of the reasons and purposes for my survival from the prison camp was for me to live and be able to be a witness in the U.S. Congress -where order and principles, and human rights are cherished - to what I experienced and saw regarding the lives of the North Koreans who live without any rights,

The fact that I am sitting before you is the sole reason why I had to survive the political prison camp of North Korea, and again I thank Ms. Suzanne Scholte for allowing my wish to come true.

———

Mr. SMITH. Ms. Kim, without a doubt, your message has been heard, and thank you for sharing what can only be described as enormous suffering that you have experienced, being sold into sexual slavery, the loss of family members, and so there will be positive consequences for your testimony. We will work hard to promote human rights in North Korea, I can assure you of that.

Before going to Mr. Scarlatoiu, I would just note I have a bill on the floor right this minute. It is the reauthorization of the Combating Autism Act of 2011. So I will leave briefly, but, without objection, Mr. Payne has graciously said that he will take the committee now.

Ms. SCHOLTE. Congressman, I just want to say, this is a map that she drew of the camp she was in.

Mr. PAYNE. We will now hear from our final witness.

STATEMENT OF MR. GREG SCARLATOIU, EXECUTIVE DIRECTOR, COMMITTEE FOR HUMAN RIGHTS IN NORTH KOREA

Mr. SCARLATOIU. Good afternoon, Mr. Payne and Ms. Bass. Thank you for inviting me to speak with you today about the human rights situation in North Korea and about the apparent increase in the amount of information getting into that country. It is an honor and a privilege to have the opportunity to discuss these issues with you today.

Mr. Payne, I would like to begin by informing you that I will be presenting a brief summary of the views included in my prepared statement.

Mr. PAYNE. Thank you. Without objection.

Mr. SCARLATOIU. After the very emotional and comprehensive testimony by Ms. Scholte, after the heartbreaking testimony by Ms. Kim Young Soon and Ms. Kim Hye Sook, there is barely anything I can add on the human rights situation in North Korea. The human rights situation in North Korea remains abysmal.

According to experts and testimony by recent North Korean defectors, there is no evidence that the human rights situation in North Korea has improved as the Kim regime proceeds with steps toward leadership succession. On the contrary, it appears the border crackdown aimed at preventing North Koreans from defecting to China has intensified, and the political prisoner camp population has been on the increase.

In May of this year, Amnesty International released satellite imagery and new testimony shedding light on the horrific conditions in North Korea's political prisoner camps. According to that organization, the prisoner population detained at such camps is up to 200,000; and a comparison of the latest satellite photos with satellite imagery from 2001 indicates a considerable increase in the scale of the camps.

Moving on to the flow of information getting into North Korea, although officially all personal radios must have a fixed dial and be registered with state security offices, programming by stations, including Voice of America, Radio Free Asia, and broadcasters based in South Korea may have a listenership of around 30 percent in North Korea.

The number of radios smuggled from China has been on the increase. The North Korean authorities continue to attempt to jam foreign broadcasting but face serious limitations in their efforts as jamming is energy intensive and North Korea is experiencing endemic energy shortages.

In recent years, we have found out that there has been a significant increase in the amount of information entering North Korea. This development is the result of the marketization that has taken place in that country. Such marketization is by no means an intended top-down reform program but, rather, a function of state failure. Small, informal markets provide ordinary people a coping mechanism that enables them to survive.

During the informal marketization of North Korea, supply chains have developed from China to North Korea's capital city of Pyongyang; and MP3 players, CD–ROMs, DVDs, and thumb drives have been entering North Korea. Statistical data, including a 2010 survey of North Korean refugees and travelers by the Broadcasting Board of Governors, indicate that 27 percent of respondents have listened to foreign radio, 48 percent have come in contact with foreign DVDs and other video material, while 27 percent have watched foreign TV.

Information is also being passed from one member to the next along such supply chains. It appears that the "Korean Wave," consisting of South Korean soap opera and music, exceptionally popular elsewhere in Asia and beyond, has also reached North Korea. According to Japan's Asahi Shimbun, one member of a group of nine North Koreans who recently sailed for 5 days before being picked up off the west coast of Japan 1 week ago on September 13, this gentleman, a squid fisherman, said that he was inspired to leave his home by South Korean soap operas.

In January, 2008, Egyptian company Orascom Telecom Holding was awarded a license to establish a 3G mobile network in North Korea. When launched in December, 2008, Koryolink had 5,300 subscribers. In its half-year earnings report for January-June, 2011, published on August 10, Orascom stated the number of subscribers in North Korea had reached 660,000.

Separate from the expansion of the Koryolink network, citizens of North Korea have also been using Chinese cellular phones smuggled across the border into North Korea.

We have indication that Koryolink intends to launch 3G Internet service via Apple iPad in Pyongyang this fall by a special SIM card. Nevertheless, Internet access is likely to continue to be restricted to foreign residents and those close to the Kim regime. There are also those North Koreans who possess computers not connected to the Web, and they are estimated to represent about 3 percent of the entire population.

Based on data collected through interviews with North Korean defectors and the proven track record of success in winning the ideological confrontation during the Cold War, radio broadcasting will continue to be one of the few media available to grant the people of North Korea access to information from the outside world. Computers not connected to the Internet, thumb drives, DVDs, CD–ROMs, and MP3 players have become increasingly available, although access to such devices is still relatively limited. Efforts to increase the flow of the information into North Korea should take into account the increasing availability of such vehicles.

I wish to thank the subcommittee and its staff for the opportunity to testify before you today, and I would now be pleased to try to answer any questions that you might have.

Thank you very much.

[The prepared statement of Mr. Greg Scarlatoiu follows:]

Testimony of Greg Scarlatoiu
Executive Director of the Committee for Human Rights in North Korea (HRNK)

Before the House Committee on Foreign Affairs
Subcommittee on Africa, Global Health, and Human Rights
September 20, 2011

"Human Rights in North Korea: Challenges and Opportunities"

Good afternoon, Chairman Smith, Mr. Payne, and members of the Subcommittee. Thank you for inviting me to speak with you today about the human rights situation in North Korea, as that country prepares for a second hereditary transmission of top leadership, and about the apparent increase in the amount of information getting into North Korea. It is an honor and privilege to have an opportunity to discuss these issues with you today.

After North Korean leader Kim Jong-il allegedly suffered a stroke in the summer of 2008, the Kim regime proceeded with preparations for third generation succession. In September 2010, one day ahead of a rare Workers' Party of Korea conference in Pyongyang, Kim Jong-il's third son, Kim Jong-un, was made a *daejang*, the equivalent to an American Four-Star General. Kim Jong-un's selection as one of the two Vice-Chairmen of North Korea's National Defense Commission and the Workers' Party Central Military Commission appears to confirm that he has been designated to succeed Kim Jong-il as leader of North Korea. According to experts, should Kim Jong-un become North Korea's leader, it is likely that Kim Jong-un's uncle Chang Sung-taek will act as a regent in the early stages, as Kim Jong-il's third son is still too young and inexperienced.

In April 2012, North Korea will celebrate the 100th birthday of its founder, "eternal president" Kim Il-sung, who died in 1994. The Kim regime has stated its goal of turning North Korea into a "strong and prosperous nation" *(kangsong-daekuk)* by the year 2012. The year 2012 may provide North Korea with an opportunity to take some significant steps towards the accomplishment of hereditary succession. The year 2012 will also mark possible changes in countries of key importance to North Korea: presidential elections will be held in March in Russia, in October in the People's Republic of China, in November in the United States, and in December in South Korea. Changes affecting the Lower House and the government may also be expected in Japan during the year 2012.

According to experts and testimony by recent North Korean defectors, there is no evidence that the human rights situation in North Korea has improved as the Kim regime proceeds with steps towards leadership succession. On the contrary, it appears that, as North Korea engaged in grave military provocations such as the sinking of the ROKS Cheonan on March 26, 2010, and the shelling of the South Korean island of Yeonpyeong on November 23, 2010, the border crackdown aimed at preventing North Koreans from defecting to China has intensified, and the political prisoner camp population has been on the increase.

The 2010 State Department Report on Human Rights Practices in North Korea, quoting *The Washington Post* and South Korea's *Donga Daily*, estimates the total number of prisoners detained in political penal-labor camps to be between 150,000 and 200,000. In May 2011, Amnesty International released satellite imagery and new testimony shedding light on the horrific conditions in North Korea's political prisoner camps. According to Amnesty International, the prisoner population detained at such camps is around 200,000, and a comparison of the latest satellite photos with satellite imagery from 2001 indicates a considerable increase in the scale of the camps. According to testimony by former inmates, many of those detained at these camps are unaware of the crimes they have allegedly committed. The majority of prisoners are held in areas inside the camps known as "Total Control Zones," where they have to be detained until they breathe their last.

In 2003, based on prisoners' testimonies and satellite imagery, the Committee for Human Rights in North Korea published one of the most comprehensive reports to date on North Korea's political prisoner camp system, entitled "The Hidden Gulag: Exposing North Korea's Prison Camps." Our organization is currently working on the second edition of "Hidden Gulag," based on information provided by North Koreans who were previously trapped in prison-labor camps. Despite North Korea's relentless denial that such camps exist, our research and interviews have revealed the detailed operation of an enormous system of arbitrary and extra-judicial detention coupled with a regime of forced labor that abuses scores of thousands of North Koreans at any one time, and has brutalized hundreds of thousands of North Koreans since the inception of this system.

Witnesses interviewed by our organization include about 60 of the hundreds of former North Koreans previously detained in the network of prison camps, penitentiaries, police detention facilities and mobile labor brigades. Their testimony and personal stories detail an extraordinary amount of unprovoked and unnecessary human suffering. This network of detention and forced labor facilities constitutes the North Korean "gulag," appropriating the common name for the Stalinist prison-labor camps of the former Soviet Union.

Despite the political oppression affecting the overwhelming majority of North Koreans, more information from the outside world appears to be making its way into the world's most reclusive nation. Although, officially, all personal radios must have a fixed dial and be registered with state security offices, programming by stations including Voice of America, Radio Free Asia and broadcasters based in South Korea may have a listenership of around 30% in North Korea. The number of radio sets smuggled from China has been on the increase. The North Korean authorities continue to attempt to jam foreign broadcasting, but face serious limitations in their efforts, as jamming is energy-intensive and North Korea is experiencing endemic energy shortages.

In recent years, we have also found out that there has been a significant increase in the amount of information entering North Korea via channels other than radio waves. This development is mostly the result of the marketization that has taken place in North Korea. Such marketization is by no means an intended top-down reform program, but rather a function of state failure. Mr. Kim Kwang-jin, a former high-ranking North Korean official who defected to South Korea, also a former visiting scholar and current non-resident fellow of our organization, has spoken about North Korea's "three economies:" the centrally planned state economy, which is in a virtual state of collapse; the "palace economy," operating in the range of hundreds of million a dollars a year, employing North Korea's military-industrial complex to earn the Kim regime the foreign currency needed to procure luxury goods and maintain its grip on power; and the "people's economy," much smaller by comparison, operating through informal markets to provide ordinary people a coping mechanism enabling them to survive.

During the informal marketization of North Korea, supply chains have developed from China to North Korea's capital city of Pyongyang, and MP3 players, CD-ROMs, DVDs and thumb drives have been entering North Korea along these supply chains. Statistical data included in a 2010 survey of North Korean refugees and travelers by the Broadcasting Board of Governors indicate that 27% of respondents have listened to foreign radio, 48% have come in contact with foreign DVDs and other video material, while 27% have watched foreign TV. The same survey indicates that 74% of North Koreans have access to TV sets, 46% to DVD players, 16% to computers, and 8% to MP3 players. A subsequent study conducted by the BBG indicates that computer thumb drives are becoming increasingly popular, but are not yet as common as MP3 players. Such data imply access, and not ownership or in-home access to such devices.

Due to severe restrictions imposed not only on travel outside North Korea, but also inside that country, the majority of the defectors come from the border regions with China, such as the North Hamgyong Province. For that and other reasons, statistical data collected by the BBG or other organizations through defector interviews are not necessarily representative of the North Korean population generally, or the North Korean refugee population in China.

In addition to contributing to the increase in the flow of information into North Korea through the introduction of new electronic devices, another side effect of these informal supply chains is that information is also being passed from one member to the next along the chain. It appears that the "Korean Wave" (called *Hallyu* in South Korea and *Nampoong*, or "Southern Wind" in North Korea), including South Korean soap operas, other TV series, music and fashion, popular elsewhere in Asia and beyond, has also reached North Korea, in particular the capital city of Pyongyang, although the percentage of those aware of the "Korean Wave" is difficult to determine.

In January 2008, Egyptian company Orascom Telecom Holding was awarded a license to establish a 3G mobile network in North Korea. When Koryolink, North Korea's cellular phone network was launched in December 2008, it had 5,300 subscribers. According to data released by Orascom, Koryolink's parent company, North Korea's cellular phone network reached 535,133 users in the January-March period of 2011, up from 431,919 users in the final quarter of 2010. On a year-to-year basis, the number of subscribers among North Korea's 24 million people represented a jump of 420 percent from 125,661 in the first quarter of 2010. According to Orascom, during the first quarter of 2011, while the number of subscribers was on the increase, average monthly cell phone usage decreased from 316 minutes in the last quarter of 2010 to 270. On a year-to-year basis, the decrease constituted a drop of 41 minutes compared to an average 311 minutes during the first quarter of 2010. While Orascom officials including Aldo Mareuse, the company's Chief Financial Officer, have interpreted the decrease in average cell phone usage as the result of "lower income segments" entering the market, other experts disagree, and point out that half a million out of a population of 24 million is still a low percentage, and it is likely that cell phones are still only in the hands of those close to the Kim regime. In its half-year earnings report for January-June 2011, published on August 10th, Orascom stated that the number of subscribers in North Korea had reached 660,000.

Separate from the expansion of the Koryolink network, citizens of North Korea have also been using Chinese cellular phones smuggled across the border into North Korea. Media organizations and NGOs in South Korea have even recruited North Koreans living inside North Korea as informants. The South Korean press and other media organizations including *The New York Times* have reported that, using Chinese cellular phones in areas of North Korea where a signal is available, a handful of North Koreans assume great risks to overcome North Korea's near-total news blackout. Given that the level of political access these sources have is rather limited, the information they provide is not necessarily useful in understanding the inner workings of the Kim regime, but it offers valuable insights into everyday life in the world's most secluded nation.

A group of experts that has recently traveled to North Korea was told by Koryolink representatives that 3G internet service via Apple iPad will be made available in Pyongyang this fall via a special SIM card developed by Koryolink. Nevertheless, internet access is likely to continue to be restricted to foreign residents and those close to the Kim regime. The percentage of North Koreans possessing computers not connected to the web is estimated to be around 3% of the entire population.

Because the North Korean people are so restricted in the information they receive about their own country and the outside world, the Committee for Human Rights in North Korea has recommended that the United States should continue to expand radio broadcasting into North Korea and encourage other efforts that provide information directly to the North Korean people in accordance with the North Korea Human Rights Act. Our Committee has also recommended that the United States should make known to the North Korean people that their welfare is of great concern to the American people.

Based on data collected through interviews with North Korean defectors and the proven track record of success in winning the ideological confrontation during the Cold War, radio broadcasting will likely continue to be one of the few media available to grant the people of North Korea access to information from the outside world. In addition to radios smuggled from China, computers not connected to the internet, thumb drives, DVDs, CD-ROMs and MP3 players have become increasingly available, although access to such devices is still relatively limited. Efforts to increase the flow of information into North Korea may benefit from taking into account the increasing availability of such vehicles.

Thank you, Mr. Chairman, Mr. Payne, and members of the Subcommittee. I look forward to answering any questions you might have.

Mr. PAYNE. Thank you very much.

Let me once again thank each of the witnesses. Your testimony is certainly very compelling. We, of course, have heard and we try to keep up with the situation in North Korea, but it certainly brings it home when we have a hearing and to hear especially from individuals who have lived through the horrors of this regime; and, of course, we appreciate our experts from the Defense Forum Foundation and the Committee for Human Rights in North Korea.

Perhaps to either one of you who are working with organizations that deal with that, Mrs. Scholte or Mr. Scarlatoiu, the special envoy for North Korea human rights, Ambassador Robert King, has said that the United States Government would engage in an indepth dialogue on human rights issues at the Six-Party Talks. The Six-Party Talks are at an impasse.

The absence of Six-Party Talks—first of all, what do each of you feel that the Six-Party Talks have achieved in the past and whether there were any real gains forward, first of all? But, secondly, if, indeed, you feel that it is an impasse or there is really not a real effort on the part of North Korea, what other fora would the Obama administration consider employing for human rights dialogue with Pyongyang? So whether talks past, and they have been going on for a bit through several administrations, and if they are scrapped, in absence of that, could there be anything else or should we continue with these? Could I ask each one of you if you would like to comment.

Ms. SCHOLTE. Well, first of all, I think that, regarding the Six-Party Talks, this was an effort by the Bush administration to rein in North Korea's nuclear ambitions, and they made the decision that they would just focus on the nuclear issue and not address any of the human rights concerns. They kicked the human rights concerns down the road.

We can tell by history that North Koreans are brilliant at manipulating the talks and using talks to gain aid and support, make promises they never intend to keep. They did the same thing to Bill Clinton during the Agreed Framework, and I think former President Clinton could be excused for that because he was dealing with a new dictator when he was President. But the Bush administration I think should have known better. They should have known the history of how this regime uses talks.

What you have seen during these talks, the result has been North Korea has developed nuclear weapons. It is very active in the proliferation of nuclear weapons, and exactly the purpose of these talks was never realized. But, at the same time, millions of North Koreans have died. And so I think that talking with this regime is useless. They only use these talks to extract concessions and support and legitimize the regime.

I think, instead, we need to take a new approach. I think President Obama is in a unique position to do that.

I think that we should make human rights the number one policy of our Government. I think that we should reach out to the North Korean people. I think that President Obama should be talking about the fact that—I think we should say we want to give North Korea as much aid as they need so that the people are not starving, but we want to be able to see that it is consumed. I think we should be talking about the fact that we want to help the people. We want to improve conditions there. We would like to see the International Red Cross go to political prisoner camps.

North Korea denies they have any camps. Well, fine, let's let an independent agency like the International Red Cross go to these camps.

And I think that we need to be focusing on the human rights issues in our policy but, at the same time, doing everything we can to support the kind of creative things that the defectors themselves are doing in radio broadcasting and these balloon launches. Because the impact that Free North Korea Radio had, which went on Internet broadcast in 2004 and then went on shortwave in 2006, the impact that Free North Korea Radio had was amazing. It set the pace for all the broadcasters because it was the defectors themselves.

And as you know, the North Koreans are raised to believe that South Korea and the United States caused the Korean War. They are brainwashed with stuff that we would think was completely ridiculous, but they believe this. So when the North Koreans themselves are talking and broadcasting these views and these opinions into North Korea, North Koreans can't dismiss them. So it has had a tremendous impact, and I think we have to be doing everything we can to reach out with that message to the North Korean people and using the defectors especially.

Mr. SCARLATOIU. Mr. Payne, the main reason why nothing has been happening on the Six-Party Talks front for a while now is that North Korea has refused to act as a responsible member of the international community.

North Korea has continued to proceed with missile nuclear developments. North Korea engaged in very serious provocations last year. In March, it launched a torpedo attack on the South Korean corvette, the Cheonan. Forty-six South Korean sailors were killed in that attack. As you have already mentioned, on November 23, North Korea shelled South Korean territory, the South Korean island of Yeonpyeong, and this attack resulted in military and civilian casualties.

We have already heard about assassins sent to kill Mr. Park Sang-hak, one of the very active North Korea defectors in South Korea, a few weeks back. There were deep concerns about an alleged assassination plot targeting Mr. Kim Kwan-jin, the defense minister of South Korea. And before the most high-profile North Korean defector, Mr. Hwang Jang-yop, passed away late last year, only few months before that we heard about a plot that was targeting him for assassination.

That being said, North Korea has also continued to oppress its own people. North Korea has continued to refuse to abide by the international obligations that it is supposed to abide by, given it is a party to the international Covenant on Civil and Political Rights; the international Covenant on Economic, Social, and Cultural Rights; the International Convention against All Forms of Discrimination against Women; the International Convention on the Rights of the Child; and, as a U.N. member state, it is supposed to be bound by the U.N. Universal Declaration on Human Rights.

As to whether human rights should be on the agenda, it is the firm belief of the Committee for Human Rights in North Korea that human rights, the improvement of the human rights situation in North Korea should be at the top of our priorities; and, personally, as I hope that one day we will see the complete, irreversible, and verifiable dismantlement of North Korea's nuclear program, I also hope that we will see the complete, irreversible, and verifiable dismantlement of North Korea's political prisoner camps as well.

Mr. PAYNE. Thank you very much.

Let me ask you, Ms. Kim Young Soon, or you, Ms. Kim Hye Sook, there is—and I know that your experiences in North Korea were years ago and you have very compelling testimony. I am just curious to know, in your days as a young person, as a child, as a teenager, as a young adult growing up, what type of society, what type of programs does the government impose on children?

You know, it is supposed to be a time of life when people are happy. They are growing and learning. To your best recollection, could you, if you can, explain what is life like for a young child and a young teenager, young adult growing up in North Korea today, if you can sort of transpose your experiences.

Ms. KIM YOUNG SOON. Congressman, in answer to your question, after the liberation from Japan in 1945 and until the 1970s, North Korea was actually a little bit better—was actually better than South Korea in terms of the economic situation.

And as for myself, when I was young, I went to school and I attended the university, Pyongyang University of Fine Arts, and I majored in dance. I learned under the teachings of a very well-known North Korean dancer. And before I went to Yoduk prison camp, I can say with assurance that I was very happy, that my happiness quotient, so to speak, was very high in terms of living in North Korean society.

Mr. PAYNE. Thank you.

Ms. KIM HYE SOOK. Congressman, for my case, before I was sent away to Bukchang prison camp, I had a life where I had no worries about food, about eating. I went to school. I lived a normal life. But because I was sent to prison camp at such an early age, that is all about that I can share about in terms of my experience in relation to your question.

Mr. PAYNE. Thank you.

One other question that I was just curious about. As we do know that in World War II there was the question of the brothels that were created in Korea, and I wonder whether it was in the north of Korea or was that primarily in Korea itself, if anyone recalls.

As you may know, we are still working on a real apology from the Government of Japan. There has been some apologies, but this has been an issue that has plagued the world since that time. I wonder whether it was prevalent throughout Korea.

Ms. KIM YOUNG SOON. My answer to you, sir, is that before liberation in—before the liberation in 1945, even in the northern part of the peninsula, North Korea, there were incidents or places where these comfort women stationed on locations were based in North Korea, and I believe that even if this issue were to be addressed with the Japanese Government we would not be getting a satisfactory answer or clear answer from the Japanese Government in regard to your question, sir.

Mr. PAYNE. Thank you.

I yield to the gentlelady from California.

Ms. BASS. Thank you very much, Mr. Chair.

I actually would like to follow up on a question that Mr. Payne said to Ms. Soon and Ms. Sook about your childhood until you went into the camps. And, Ms. Soon, you said up until the 1970s—and I realize that is when you went into the camps—but did things drastically change in North Korea and when?

Ms. KIM YOUNG SOON. To answer your question, Kim Il Sung's propaganda was set in place between the years of liberation and until the Korean War. Those years were known as the best years in terms of the affluence and prosperity of North Korea.

After the Korean War, there were various economic trends that were instituted to try to help the economy and to help the people live better. But, in 1987—in the late 1980s, after the Soviet Union collapsed and after the help from that part of the region stopped, that is what brought on the change in terms of the economic downturn and the conditions for the people in North Korea.

Ms. BASS. I see.

First of all, let me also just thank you for coming and sharing your testimony. I think it is very, very important that people in this country hear and learn what is going on in North Korea, because I don't think much is known here about what is happening there. And the pain and the suffering that you have described, the loss of your family members, not knowing where your children are, your husband, you know, is just—I think it is an immeasurable amount of pain, and I appreciate you taking the time and sharing that with us.

I think it is especially important because the need for foreign aid and the need for assistance—and I am sorry, I don't want to mispronounce your name—Ms. Sook, when you talked about the need for there to be foreign assistance and food and all in times when we are talking about cutting back. So I think the message is critically important.

But, Ms. Sook, you were saying that you thought that we shouldn't have discussions, negotiations with North Korea, but, at the same time, we should do what we can to, you know, deliver food and other things that the population would need. How do we do that? I understand the communication part, funding, but how would we get aid to people? How would we get aid to the people that need it?

If Ms. Soon could answer it first, Ms. Soon or Ms. Sook, that would be great.

Ms. KIM YOUNG SOON. I would like to say that the world is supporting North Korea because they hear stories of people starving and suffering. But, as a North Korean defector, I believe that the regime of North Korea should be completely isolated, and that is the only way to change the regime. And unless North Korea adopts a market economy and changes drastically the way it—the way the country is run, nothing—no change will come. And, as a defector, I would like to say that real help would be for the Kim Jong Il regime to be completely isolated and stop the aid that is being given to the regime.

Ms. BASS. Weren't you calling for something different?

Ms. SCHOLTE. Actually, I agree, except I was just making the point that if we are going—I actually believe in a substantial amount of assistance but only if we can stay to the point of consumption. Because if the relief—if we send any amount of assistance to North Korea, it will be diverted. And when you talk to defectors, they never saw any food aid; and when you talk to defectors that serve in the military, they will tell you the World Food Programme rolls into town, delivers rice to these families. Right after they leave, the army comes back and takes it all back.

In fact, there was a Dr. Norbert Vollertsen who testified some years ago about how he had gone to an orphanage and they had handed out cookies, and the kids just sat there with the cookie waiting for somebody to come back and take it away.

So the diversion has been absolute; and, because of that, I think that that is the kind of a message that we could send that would be a very powerful message for positive propaganda, which is that we very much are concerned about the starvation and the political prisoner camps and the situation in North Korea. We want to help you. We hear about these stories. We want to help you, but we want to be sure that we are actually helping the people. And we are only going to give that aid if we know we can stay there.

Even from the very beginning when the famine first started, North Korea put such stipulations on the food aid. They actually didn't want—I have never heard of this before, but—I have never heard about this before—and challenge me on this—but I don't think of any situation where there is a country where there was starvation, where the country that was the intended recipient of the aid demanded that the aid deliverers couldn't speak their language. I don't think that has ever happened in any place but North Korea. Because usually if you are going into a country to deliver aid, you are desperate for somebody who speaks the language. But that just speaks volumes about just from the very beginning of their intention to divert aid.

So because of the difficulty of preventing aid from being diverted, that is why I say we should only provide aid if we can be there at the point of consumption.

I could tell you all kinds of stories, but if we were to go in an orphanage and deliver formula, we have got to make sure those babies get that formula. Because Action Against Hunger did that, and that formula ended up in Pyongyang in the markets, and those babies were given watered-down goats' milk when they showed up a month later to find out what happened to the tons of baby food it had delivered to that orphanage. That is just one example.

But I think that—and then the second point I was making is that we should be looking at creative ways to get in information, like radio broadcasting but also through the balloon launches and also through the North Koreans that have defected that are sending in remittances into the country that are helping support their families.

Ms. BASS. Thank you very much.

Mr. PAYNE. Thank you.

The chairman has returned, so I will give the chair back to him and hold any questions I have until a later time.

Mr. Chairman.

Mr. SMITH. I want to thank Ranking Member Payne for leading the committee. Again, I had to leave because a bill of mine on autism was on the floor; and it did pass, thankfully.

Let me just ask a question, if I could, a few years back in 2002, in May, I chaired a hearing on North Korea human rights, one of several; and we had Dr. Norbert Vollertsen, a former medical doctor inside of North Korea, who actually was given a huge award by the dictatorship for his medical expertise and the fact that he helped cure a whole lot of people. But he also then told the truth about the human rights situation, and he said that they are using food as a weapon—talking about the dictatorship—against their own people. They are committing genocide, and I think we have to care. As an international community, we have to intervene.

Ms. Scholte, would you say—that was in 2002—that the international community—and I heard in your opening comments that you had criticism that Bush did not focus on human rights nor did Bill Clinton in North Korea. We did pass the North Korea Human Rights Act. I was one of the cosponsors of that bill. Jim Leach was the prime sponsor. It was an excellent bill. Mr. Payne—all of us—strongly supported it. Has that legislation lived up to its promise? Are we emphasizing human rights sufficiently in our dialogue or whatever it is of a dialogue with the North Koreans?

Ms. SCHOLTE. I would say I have been actually very disappointed after all the hard work we did in getting the North Korea Human Rights Act passed. I have been very disappointed right from the very start. The Bush administration said we welcome these tools that you are giving us to help on this issue, but then they never really used those tools.

The one thing it did help I know with radio broadcasting and expanding VOA and RFA support, which was really I believe as a result of that legislation, was a huge—one huge, great thing, factor, that happened with the radio broadcasting. That is so important, and also helping like Free North Korea Radio, some of the independent broadcasters.

The other thing, though, too, is the special envoy position. I think it is very significant that President Obama has made it very clear that his special envoy, Robert King, will be part of all discussions and negotiation on North Korea. That was not the case during the Bush administration. Jay Lefkowitz was cut out. So I think that President Obama is taking greater advantage of that legislation to try to do more with the North Korean rights act just by the very nature of the way he has elevated Ambassador King's position.

On the comment you made about North Korea using food as a weapon, that is absolutely true. It uses food as a weapon against its own people, and they have an apartheid system in North Korea where people are classified based on loyalty to the regime. You have the elites. Then you have what they consider the wavering class, which is the class that is not considered to be completely loyal to the regime, and then you have got the hostile class. And if you are in the elites you may get white rice, but if you are down on that classification system, you may never see any rice your whole life. You may get corn.

But the thing that has happened with the food is, because of the breakdown in the public distribution system which is how the regime rewarded people through this apartheid-type system based on loyalty, that system has broken down. That is why these markets are so significant, that you have over 200 markets, and these are just the ones we know—can identify by satellite. These are just the ones we know by satellite. There are probably many more markets. But that is how people are surviving. They are trading and selling and buying among themselves in these markets.

Mr. SMITH. If either or both of our Kims could comment, Ms. Kim and Ms. Kim, on, one, the use of torture in the gulags. We have had testimony before this committee in the past that Christians and people of faith are even more selected out for repression especially, and women who are pregnant are often forcibly aborted in an absolutely crude—they get beaten around the abdomen and then miscarry. So it is a horrible thing. We had testimony of boards being put on women and soldiers or gulag security guards jumping on the boards on the abdomen of the pregnant women.

Did you experience torture? And you mentioned how both of you, you saw littered bodies everywhere, that people were treated like animals.

Ms. Kim, you said that, "A society where the whole country is a prison. A society where those who escaped the country in search of freedom were caught and imprisoned and executed and where those who have escaped become lost people and orphans in the international community. A society where chastity and virginity, which is more precious than life, is sold cheaper than the cheapest of things." Of course talking about the scourge of human trafficking. If you could speak to the use of torture and these terrible and despicable atrocities being committed by the dictatorship.

Ms. KIM YOUNG SOON. In answer to your question, regarding my experience at Yoduk, before I was sent to Yoduk, during the 2 months of interrogation, I was stuck in a room with no calendar, no clock, really a black hole for 2 months. And for somebody to come out of that and not go crazy, it is a miracle, and that is what I experienced.

And in terms of actually being in Yoduk and my experience there, I saw violence—inmate-on-inmate violence. I was injured in my shoulder during work and also my fingers were injured during work. And in terms of torture, the violence, that is what I experienced during my prison experience at Yoduk prison camp.

Mr. SMITH. Ms. Kim.

Ms. KIM HYE SOOK. Regarding my experience, to answer your question, you could see in some of the drawings that I displayed what I went through.

But at prison camp number 18 there was no paved road, and there were many times where the prison guards would force prisoners—would stop these prisoners walking back and forth from work within the camp. They would stop these prisoners, force them to open their mouths, and these prisoners would—these prison guards would spit—spit the phlegm into the mouths—open mouths of prisoners. They would tell them if you swallow it you will not be beaten, but if you throw up or resist you will be relentlessly beaten.

I experienced that torture a total of times during my 28 years there. And in 2005—in 2005 when I—after I was released from camp and I was caught—I went into China, was caught and repatriated, during the detention period when I was going through that, I saw an incident where women who were also caught and repatriated were forced through repeated sitting and standing up action so that anything they were hiding in their uterus would fall out, hidden money or other contraband that the prison guards were trying to find.

So that is the extent of the torture I witnessed from my time in North Korea.

Mr. SMITH. Mr. Scarlatoiu, you indicate in your testimony that there is evidence that human rights abuses in North Korea are intensifying as the regime takes steps toward leadership succession. Could you speak further on that issue and perhaps some of the evidence that you have that suggests that?

Mr. SCARLATOIU. Mr. Chairman, I should tell you that our organization has published one quite well-known report on the political prisoner camps in North Korea called Hidden Gulag. That happened in 2003. We are now in the process of putting together a second edition; and, toward that goal, we have collected testimony by at least about 60 former inmates of political prisoner camps. The difference between now and then is that we have had testimony from some guards. We have better satellite imagery.

Based on such testimony, we seem to see intensified political repression, we seem to see a crackdown along the border with China, and all indications are that the new center nucleus of power being created around the third son of Kim Jong Il, around Kim Jong Un, is not composed of any type of reformists. We have all indications, including violent provocations against South Korea, violent military provocations, dispatching of assassins, intensified human rights violations in North Korea. We have all evidence that we are dealing with very hard-liners.

Mr. SMITH. Let me ask a question with regards to Juche. I read a book some years back about the self-reliance religion and the cult of personality, the deification of Kim Jong Il and Kim Il Sung before him, and it was a very detailed, heavily footnoted book with how they brainwash the people of North Korea. And I am wondering if all of you might speak to this and especially the two Kims. How did they overcome this brainwashing effort? Do people in North Korea really regard Kim Jong Il as good?

There was a National Geographic piece on recently, and I watched it with great interest. I watched it more than once. And a doctor went to North Korea to do some surgeries on the eye, and he was having phenomenal success teaching other doctors and practitioners in North Korea to do so. But I was astonished how the people who had been helped, especially at a group meeting, were looking at a picture of Kim Jong Il and thanking him and getting on their knees and worshiping him.

And the intensity of it was quite unnerving, frankly, and I am wondering how they deny people information. They jam obviously outside broadcasts, but this brainwashing obviously starts from the moment a child can speak and talk and hear, I should say, and I am wondering how they overcame that. Was what we saw on that video true, that he is regarded as a god?

Ms. KIM YOUNG SOON. I would like to answer your question by saying that in North Korea from basically childbirth, from kindergarten on, little children are brainwashed into believing that Kim Il Sung, Kim Jong Il are capable of superhuman accomplishments and that there are not enough words to praise, not enough words in the world to praise Kim Il Sung and Kim Jong Il, and they are so brainwashed that there is no room whatsoever in their minds to think otherwise in North Korea.

And the people in North Korea, it is a situation where their minds have been replaced with a brainwashed mind, and there is no freedom to travel to countries where you need special color-coded passes to travel to a particular place, and it is a nation—society where hands and feet are tied of the people so that they cannot travel or be free in that society.

Ms. KIM HYE SOOK. To answer your question, from my experience, as soon as you are born in North Korea you are taught phrases: Thank you, dear leader; thank you, great leader.

And one example I would like to give you, sir, is that in 2009 when I escaped to China there was a woman with a young daughter who accompanied me, and the Chinese family that was helping us gave this starving child food, and the first words out of the child's mouth when she received the food was, thank you, dear leader, Kim Jong Il. So that goes to show you the extent of the brainwashing.

And in North Korea from the moment you are born until the day you die, thank you, dear leader, Kim Jong Il; thank you great leader, Kim Il Sung, those words are just brainwashed into the people's minds.

Mr. SMITH. Thank you.

Just a few final questions and then—did you want—yes, Ms. Scholte.

Ms. SCHOLTE. I just wanted to add one comment. That is one of the things about this whole idea——

There was a woman I met who had been a defector, and she had taught philosophy. So I casually asked her, oh, who is your favorite philosopher, you know, and she was like, oh, I only taught Kim Il Sungism and Marxism for the first 10 years of my career, and then for the last 10 years, just Kim Jong Ilism. And I said, well, when you got free to South Korea, did you pursue philosophy? And she said, no, I was afraid that my brain was too twisted to be able to understand that.

And I thought the fact that she admitted that proved that it wasn't, that she—her brain had opened up, but she was actually studying North Korean studies to figure out a way to help her country.

But I want to say one of the programs that Free North Korea Radio is trying to do—and we are actually reaching out to the Christian churches to help us. We want to do a program explaining the concept of, you know, when we think of religious faith and self-sacrifice and helping others versus what they are brainwashed to believe, to try to help North Koreans kind of open them to understanding the concepts that we have got in the Western world, which is serving others and helping others, which is a complete opposite of everything that they are taught, which is they are the servants of the regime.

That is one of the things that I think is really important, because the defectors know how to articulate those kinds of things.

And another thing, too, there is an organization called the Coalition for North Korea Women's Solidarity, and this is a coalition formed by North Korean women, most of whom were victims of trafficking. But the whole concept—when they first came to South Korea, the whole concept of human rights is completely alien to them, and you would believe that the social society is trying to say, well, that women are equal, but in North Korea women are treated horribly. So this is something that they are doing to help restore these women and teach them the value they are as human beings and the value they are as women. It is a very important program the defectors are taking.

Mr. SMITH. Mr. Scarlatoiu.

Mr. SCARLATOIU. I think that the brutal and ruthless dictators such as the Kims in North Korea and the cult of personality built around them depend by far and large on denying their citizens knowledge of alternative economic, social, and political systems.

You have mentioned that Christians are subject to harsh punishment. We have also come across evidence that, among those North Korean defectors forcibly repatriated from China, those who have come in contact with Christian missionaries or South Koreans face particularly harsh punishment, in some cases amounting to public executions. Most likely the main reason beyond that is that both Christianity and South Korea present alternative systems.

One great advantage that eastern Europeans had primarily through public broadcasting that they were receiving from the outside world was that it was clear to them that the capitalist, liberal democracies of the West were clearly the alternative; and I really think that we have an opportunity now to focus on improving the flow of information to North Korea, to persuade not only the overwhelming majority of North Koreans who are so oppressed but also, why not, the elites of North Korea, that there is life after the Kim regime and that alternatives are available.

Mr. SMITH. Let me just make a note here that we have asked— I have asked the administration in hearings and through other means to put China on Tier III for human trafficking, not only because of the horrific rise in sex trafficking in the People's Republic of China among Chinese but also because if a North Korean woman thinks she has gotten to relative safety and freedom by crossing the border, she invariably is sold into human trafficking. And the Chinese Government doesn't lift a single finger to mitigate her pain and to rescue her and to crack down on the traffickers who dot the border looking for women who are leaving that country.

They also violate the Refugee Convention, and China is a signatory to the Refugee Convention, because they send back men and women who are most likely to be incarcerated in the gulag, if not executed, for leaving without permission. So China bears a huge responsibility for its enabling and complicity in the crimes of Pyongyang.

Let me also ask just a final question: How would you rate the international community's response, including the U.S., Europe, and especially the United Nations? There is a high commissioner for human rights. There is a whole rapporteur system. Obviously, they have not had access in most cases to North Korea. But there is also the Human Rights Council, which was supposed to speak truth to power regardless of the consequences and hold countries to account.

Now, I frequently would, when it was a commission and now the Council, would ask the Council or commission to raise human rights in North Korea; and, frankly, there have been resolutions in the past. But it has struck me that they are almost like pro forma resolutions. They have low expectations. There is no sense of shock or dismay over what Kim Jong Il has been doing and his fellow dictators in Pyongyang. And there is that sense, you know, it is an obligatory chastisement and no one expects anything to change. And, because of those low expectations, that country in no way is held to account.

So why is the international community so incredibly passive when it comes to what is equivalent to what the Nazis did in its gulags to its own people and to Jews and to others, which is going on current day in North Korea? If you could speak to that.

And to the two Kims, finally, I was in South Korea recently, spoke to a number of lawmakers and others in Seoul, and I was kind of surprised—and maybe I am wrong in my impression—to glean from that experience that many people in South Korea don't have the kind of understanding of the two Kims that have been brought to this committee, and that is what goes on in those gulags and the huge repression that is from womb to tomb by the dictatorship. The young people kind of trivialize it in South Korea. Is that true or is that a false impression that I picked up on that trip? "We know it is there, but it is not as bad." And they just don't seem to take it at face value for the huge atrocity that it is.

So any of you who would like to speak to that.

Mr. SCARLATOIU. Chairman Smith, regarding your first question, at the Committee for Human Rights in North Korea, we are very familiar with the work and the reporting done by the U.N. special rapporteurs on the human rights situation in North Korea. Both the current rapporteur, Professor Marzuki Darusman from Indonesia, and the previous rapporteur, Professor Vitit Muntarbhorn from Thailand, are very dedicated scholars and very good human beings who have worked very hard to put together——

Mr. SMITH [continuing]. Has testified before our committee in the past.

Mr. SCARLATOIU. We are aware of that, sir—so they have done extraordinary work to shed light on the atrocities and the human rights violations happening in North Korea.

I think that organizations such as ours have a duty to inform the international community, to conduct research, to publish about the human rights violations happening in North Korea, and to engage in robust public information campaigns to inform the public here in the United States and beyond and also to inform North Koreans on the rights that they have but are being violated with such impudence.

Ms. SCHOLTE. I was going to say that you mentioned China, and I would say that there is a direct correlation between the ability of the U.N. to do anything and China stymieing those efforts.

And what you mentioned about the refugees, this is the most solvable human rights crisis that is going on in the world today. It could be solved overnight if China simply followed the treaties that it signed. The UNHCR has an office in Beijing. These refugees have a place to go. They are the only refugees I know in the world that—again, another thing that makes North Korea unique—that have a place to go. Because they are citizens under the South Korean constitution. And, of course, our North Korean Human Rights Act says that we will take some here, and people are willing to resettle them.

So there is no reason for China to continue this brutal policy of repatriation that has caused 80 percent of North Korean women to be trafficked in this basically modern-day slave markets.

And I believe you have a hearing tomorrow. One of the pressures on this is the fact that China has a shortage of women because they have been murdering unborn baby girls all these years. They have had this policy—one-child policy, and that has led to the shortage of women. So that is why young North Korean women that are vulnerable are being sold.

But China is the reason why we can't get more action at the United Nations, because they block efforts, when the Cheonan—everyone realized that North Korea had caused the death of these South Korean sailors, China was the one that was suppressing that, action on that. And so as long as you have a country like China have such tremendous influence on the U.N. that is involved in perpetrating these crimes that are happening in North Korea, you are not going to get any real action by the United Nations. Anyway, that is my—and I know you wanted to say something too.

Ms. KIM YOUNG SOON. I would like to add that the crimes against humanity committed by the Kim Jong Il regime is the worst in the world, and the United States needs to just totally isolate the regime of Kim Jong Il. The best way to go about prosecuting the crimes against humanity that Kim Jong Il has committed is to report him to the International Criminal Court. And I believe that the United States will be able to do a good job of leading an international movement work to make this—to bring about this work of bringing Kim Jong Il to the ICC, to the International Criminal Court.

And I would just like to say again that as long as Kim Jong Il is, as long as he exists, the people suffering will continue. And I would like to just say once again that my earnest desire is that the United States will take the lead in helping the world, the entire world, focus on the important issue of—focusing on human rights issue and of isolating Kim Jong Il regime and to not provide any aid or help that will only go toward keeping the regime alive.

Ms. KIM HYE SOOK. I also would like to point out, as I am sitting here before media and before the Congressman here, that regarding food aid, I would just like to point out that my younger sister and brother who are still in the prison camp, certainly all the food aid that has been given is not going to them, is not being sent to them, where the people that need it the most, the prisoners, the starving prisoners in prison would need the food aid the most, but it is only going to the elites, to the military or to the security apparatus in feeding them and empowering them, only giving them more life, more power, to continue the abuse that I drew, the drawings that you can see on display here.

Ms. SCHOLTE. Also, the attitude in South Korea, right? You asked also about the attitude in South Korea?

Mr. SMITH. South Korea, especially the young people.

Ms. SCHOLTE. I definitely think they might have a comment about that.

Mr. SMITH. It is almost like a sense of disbelief as to the scope and the cruelty of Kim Jong Il.

Ms. SCHOLTE. This is so important.

Mr. SMITH. Is it the media that has downplayed it?

Ms. SCHOLTE. That is a huge issue. That is so important, because you would think that the country that should care the most has been the slowest to respond. The reason for that is during the years of the D.J. Kim government and the Roh government, they actually banned information to be reported about what was going on in North Korea because they had the sunshine policy, which is basically an engagement policy. And the award-winning documentary Seoul Train, which is still very popular today, for example, that was produced by some Americans about the refugee crisis in China—North Koreans escaping and the whole situation—that was banned from being shown in South Korea by the government. So there was a suppression of the horrors that were going on.

They can tell you stories about—she wanted to speak before the South Korean Assembly but she wasn't able to do it, Mrs. Kim. And what has happened, though, is—oh, she was going to speak before them, okay. And they can share that with you. But what happened is with the provocations that have happened against South Korea by North Korea, unprovoked attacks, there has been an awakening in South Korea. And I am very pleased to see a lot of young people being drawn to this issue.

I have actually gone to a conference in 2002, an international conference on North Korea rights in Seoul, in which people like these defectors were going to speak, and there were students protesting against the conference. But that has changed a lot. Young people are really getting drawn to the issue. But it has been very difficult to move the hearts and souls of the Korean lawmakers. They still have not passed the North Korean Rights Act, which has been done by Japan and the United States, bipartisan. And that has been a real source of contention.

Mr. SMITH. And it brings to mind after World War II, it was Eisenhower who said, "Do not burn down the concentration camps," because there were some Germans who were in disbelief that they were real. And it seems to me that when it is an actual policy of a government to suppress the truth, there is something inherently wrong with that because it creates a distortion, a gross caricature of what Pyongyang is actually doing.

And I hope this hearing, and it will be followed by additional hearings, will further the information. I mean, I was telling, or in conversations, conveying information about what I had read and what I had learned from hearings and from defectors that had—

and my friends who are South Korean with whom I was meeting, was met with disbelief as if somehow I was exaggerating or engaging in some kind of hyperbole, when the truth on the ground as you have so borne—so ably witness to is even worse than what we could imagine in terms of the cruelty and mistreatment.

Ms. SCHOLTE. I just thought of something else I need to share with you. In October I was at a balloon launch. And I was with Kim Seong Min, Park Sang Hak, the North Korea People's Liberation Front, we were getting ready to do a balloon launch. And there was a former North Korean defector who served in the military. And he was so upset because there were these leftist South Koreans trying to stop the balloon launch and saying they were pro-Kim Jong Il. And he was so upset and almost had tears in his eyes. And he was like, I came from that country, how can they deny the horrible things that I have seen? And I remember holding him saying, Well, we don't want to get in a confrontation with them. And I said something like, I know how you feel. And I thought I don't know how he feels. That people—that he could have gone through these horrible things and then have people denying it and trying to stop him from doing something to reach out to the people who are suffering.

Ms. KIM YOUNG SOON. I would just like to add what you said, Congressman Smith, about the people in South Korea, the young people to the politicians, not fully knowing or understanding or appreciating the situation in North Korea. She wholeheartedly concurs with that statement. And because of the strong presence of the leftist and the pro-North Korean elements in South Korean society, I believe that the peninsula is not ready for unification, South Korea is not ready to be unified with North Korea. And I would again like to ask for the United States to take the lead in increasing knowledge and awareness about the situation in North Korea and help lead other nations to be able to achieve this. And there are 23,000 North Korean defectors who have resettled in South Korea.

And also there is a diaspora of North Korean defectors that are all over the world. And if there is any sort of encouragement, help, financial help, that is given to us, we will stop at nothing and we will dedicate our very lives to bring about change and the regime in North Korea. And you could trust me when I say that, Congressman Smith.

Mr. SMITH. Well, Ms. Kim, I think your point about the leftists truly enabling by either suppressing or by denying that these atrocities are occurring, that makes them complicit in these crimes against humanity. And I would hope that clear-thinking people, newspapers, and other media in South Korea will just tell the truth about what is going on in North Korea because the truth is liberating.

And I would also add my endorsement to what you said about Kim Jong Il and others being held to account for genocide at the International Criminal Court. They have committed barbaric crimes. And while there are some U.N. individuals who have spoken out, there has been no holding to account in any meaningful way. So I echo and endorse what you said.

Mr. Payne.

Mr. PAYNE. Thank you very much. I just have a quick question and I will make a little comment quickly. With the prospect of the anticipation that Kim Jong Il leaves and his son would take over, that is a horrible prospect but what do you see the consequence of something like that happening?

Ms. KIM YOUNG SOON. I believe that Kim Jong Un will never be recognized or become the true leader in North Korea. But should he, or if he were to become the next leader, I believe that there is a chance that he might open up and reform the country from her point of view and her opinion.

Mr. PAYNE. Thank you very much. I just want to comment that I think that in separated countries, like we see in Korea, the fact that much—in many instances the truth certainly is kept from the people in the south, the total truth, and it is difficult to know whose responsibility it is. Is it the government, is it the press, is it deliberate?

One thing that usually happens in divided countries, as we saw in eastern and western Europe, although you can't compare eastern Europe totally, certainly not to North Korea, but there was a strong move for reunification. It is just a natural nationalistic move to reunite countries that were once united. And so I could possibly understand why some of the younger people would be striving for unification, trying to, of course, have a change, a regime change in the north. So I think it is kind of just normal nationalism, especially a country that may have felt that it has been abused or exploited by world wars and things of that nature.

The other thing I remember clearly as I traveled through eastern Europe in the late 1960s, and I went to Poland, Germany, and Russia with some west Europeans, and saw, especially in Poland, photos of and news reels of the films taken inside of Warsaw with the Warsaw ghetto uprisings. And these were young adults, my age at that time, who could not believe how brutal their parents were when they were leading the Nazi regime. And they were talking in their own language, but I could kind of understand what the internal discussion was going on about, is this true? Almost disbelief. So I think that as we move forward I have to work with educating people to overcome some of these natural things.

I also think that we should try to become even more active in the Human Rights Council. There has been some progress made because before the U.S. joined the Council, when it was the committee before and then the Council, issues like what is happening in Syria, the brutality of Bishir on its people, some of the other issues, would never ever be raised.

And so there have been—I think because the U.S. has raised the issues, they have got to deal with them. And that is why I think it is important for us to be in the room, so that there could be answers when our allies are criticized or resolutions continually come criticizing them. We can then now say, Well, wait a minute, let me give you the other point of view.

So I do hope that those agencies will also be strengthened as we move. And then, of course, us not being a part of the Rome Statute, it makes us a little less significant in the ICC where we have difficulty pushing for indictments for war criminals who should be indicted and the cases should be raised.

The final thing I would like to say is really commend the South Korean Government. Several years ago I visited in one of my trips to Ethiopia, there is a hospital that the South Korean Government built, probably the best hospital in sub-Saharan Africa just about. And they did it because they were appreciative of the Ethiopian soldiers who fought in the Korean War. And, actually, most stunning is that for those veterans who are still alive who served, they have been paying pensions to these Ethiopian soldiers ever since the end—or, I don't know exactly if it started right at the end of the war, but for decades. And those that are still alive receive a monthly regular stipend from the Government of Korea. So I think that if some of the goodwill in southern Korea could kind of work its way up to the North, that would be a positive statement.

Thank you, Mr. Chair, for calling this very important meeting—hearing.

Mr. SMITH. Thank you, Mr. Payne.

Just to conclude, I would like to ask unanimous consent that the testimony of Kim Seong Min, Director of Free North Korea Radio, be made part of the record. Without objection, so ordered. And I would ask that all members have 5 legislative days to revise and extend remarks.

And I would just make one comment with regards to a related issue. I would like to comment on recent reports of the continued deportation of Chinese Falun Gong practitioners from South Korea to China. As is well known, the Pyongyang are brutally persecuted in China along with numerous other groups who attempt to exercise their internationally recognized human rights of freedom of thought, conscience, and religion. So I join my voice with that of other Members of Congress urging South Korea to recognize Falun Gong practitioners as refugees and not forcibly return them to China where they will certainly face persecution.

South Korea should also find an appropriate means within the South Korean legal system and the International Conventions on Torture and Refugees that it has ratified to permit these Falun Gong practitioners to remain in South Korea.

I would note that on Thursday the subcommittee will hear testimony on—it will be the 30th hearing on human rights abuses in China. It is entitled "China's One-Child Policy: The Government's Massive Crime Against Women and Unborn Babies." And I mention this, especially in light of Suzanne Scholte and others. There is a nexus between the one-child-per-couple policy. There is a dearth of females in the PRC. Estimates range to in excess of 100 million missing girls in China, so that when North Korean women make their way over the border, the traffickers are waiting to sell them into modern-day slavery and to sex trafficking. And China has not only not lifted a finger to stop it, they have enabled it. And it is attributable in part, maybe large part, to the one-child-per-couple policy.

We will hear from two victims of forced abortion who will tell their story. Chai Ling, the great Tiananmen Square activist who founded All Girls Allowed; Reggie Littejohn and Valerie Hudson who will speak about the military implications of the one-child-per-couple policy.

I do want to thank this very, very effective group of witnesses for shedding light on the egregious human rights abuses of Kim Jong Il. And thank you for bearing witness to the truth.

We need to do much more than we have done. That goes for our subcommittee, the Congress, the executive branch and the free world. And again, I want to thank all of our witnesses, especially our two women who have made their way to the U.S., come a long distance, suffered, lost loved ones for speaking truth to a very totalitarian power.

I would like to give the last word if any of our witnesses would like to say anything in conclusion.

Ms. SCHOLTE. I was just going to announce that we are having at noon on Thursday, September 22nd, a protest. We are calling on people, wherever you are in the world, to go to the Chinese Embassy at noon to protest the repatriation of North Korean refugees. And we have petitions that people are delivering. And so far we have 25 cities and 13 countries that are participating. So I just wanted to mention that.

Mr. SCARLATOIU. Mr. Chairman, I would like to tell you that in addition to one report that I have mentioned, that we have been working on on the political prisoner camps in North Korea, we are also working on a report on the circulation of information inside North Korea, and we will be happy to share these reports—as soon as they are published—with the subcommittee.

Mr. SMITH. And we will disseminate it widely among the Members of Congress, so thank you. Thank you. The hearing is adjourned and thank you very much.

[Whereupon, at 5:19 p.m., the subcommittee was adjourned.]

APPENDIX

MATERIAL SUBMITTED FOR THE HEARING RECORD

SUBCOMMITTEE HEARING NOTICE
COMMITTEE ON FOREIGN AFFAIRS
U.S. HOUSE OF REPRESENTATIVES
WASHINGTON, D.C. 20515-0128

SUBCOMMITTEE ON AFRICA, GLOBAL HEALTH, AND HUMAN RIGHTS
Christopher H. Smith (R-NJ), Chairman

September 14, 2011

You are respectfully requested to attend an OPEN hearing of the Committee on Foreign Affairs, to be held by the Subcommittee on Africa, Global Health, and Human Rights, to be held in **Room 2172 of the Rayburn House Office Building (and available live, via the WEBCAST link on the Committee website at http://www.hcfa.house.gov):**

DATE: Tuesday, September 20, 2011

TIME: 3:00 p.m.

SUBJECT: Human Rights in North Korea: Challenges and Opportunities

WITNESSES: Ms. Suzanne Scholte
                   President
                   Defense Forum Foundation

                   Ms. Kim Young Soon
                   Vice President
                   Committee for the Democratization of North Korea

                   Ms. Kim Hye Sook
                   Longest–serving survivor of North Korean prison camps

                   Mr. Greg Scarlatoiu
                   Executive Director
                   Committee for Human Rights in North Korea

By Direction of the Chairman

The Committee on Foreign Affairs seeks to make its facilities accessible to persons with disabilities. If you are in need of special accommodations, please call 202/225-5021 at least four business days in advance of the event, whenever practicable. Questions with regard to special accommodations in general (including availability of Committee materials in alternative formats and assistive listening devices) may be directed to the Committee.

COMMITTEE ON FOREIGN AFFAIRS

MINUTES OF SUBCOMMITTEE ON _____*Africa, Global Health, and, Human Rights*_____ HEARING

Day _____*Tuesday*_____ Date _____*September 20, 2011*_____ Room _____*2172 Rayburn*_____

Starting Time _____*3:00 p.m.*_____ Ending Time _____*5:19 p.m.*_____

Recesses ___*0*___ (____ to ____) (____ to ____) (____ to ____) (____ to ____) (____ to ____) (____ to ____)

Presiding Member(s)

Rep. Chris Smith, Rep. Don Payne

Check all of the following that apply:

Open Session ☑   Electronically Recorded (taped) ☑
Executive (closed) Session ☐   Stenographic Record ☑
Televised ☑

TITLE OF HEARING:

Human Rights in North Korea: Challenges and Opportunities

SUBCOMMITTEE MEMBERS PRESENT:

Rep. Chris Smith, Rep. Donald Payne, Rep. Tom Marino, Rep. Karen Bass

NON-SUBCOMMITTEE MEMBERS PRESENT: *(Mark with an * if they are not members of full committee.)*

Rep. Frank Wolf*

HEARING WITNESSES: Same as meeting notice attached? Yes ☑ No ☐
(If "no", please list below and include title, agency, department, or organization.)

STATEMENTS FOR THE RECORD: *(List any statements submitted for the record.)*

Prepared statement of Ms. Scholte
Prepared statement of Ms. Kim Young Soon
Prepared statement of Ms. Kim Hye Sook
Prepared statement of Mr. Scarlatoiu
Prepared statement of Mr. Kim Seong Min

TIME SCHEDULED TO RECONVENE _____
or
TIME ADJOURNED _____*5:19 p.m.*_____

Subcommittee Staff Director

MATERIAL SUBMITTED FOR THE RECORD BY THE HONORABLE CHRISTOPHER H. SMITH, A REPRESENTATIVE IN CONGRESS FROM THE STATE OF NEW JERSEY, AND CHAIRMAN, SUBCOMMITTEE ON AFRICA, GLOBAL HEALTH, AND HUMAN RIGHTS

Kim Seong Min   Director, Free North Korea Radio
September 20, 2011
House Committee on Foreign Affairs Subcommittee on Africa, Global Health and Human Rights

Hello, my name is Kim Seong Min and I am a defector who escaped from North Korea in 1997, and currently I run "Free North Korea Radio" (FNKR) in Seoul, South Korea, which is a radio station that broadcasts into North Korea. It is a great honor for me to be able to share with the honorable Members of Congress through this written testimony the activities of Free North Korea Radio and other North Korean defector groups in Seoul.

Free North Korea Radio is a radio station that was formed in April of 2004 to broadcast messages of freedom, the truth of the democratic outside world, and information regarding human rights to the people of North Korea as well as to South Korea and the United States.

At that time, during the South Korean leftist administration of Roh Moo Hyun, he acquiesced to the Kim Jong-il regime and declared the ceasing of the government-run broadcasts into North Korea that had been airing on the basis of the North Korean people's right to know of the outside world. However, because we defectors knew the importance of broadcasts into North Korea, we formed a radio station through our wish to continue the broadcasts in the private sector that which was stopped by the government, and ultimately broadcast 5 hours daily, from the initial 1 hour daily broadcasts.

We have great pride in the work we do in having established our own internal network inside North Korea and establishing a cellphone-based connection with North Korea citizens, thereby reporting the ever-changing internal news of North Korea that was carried by the well-known and major media outlets of South Korea and the world. Also, the 1,000 or so North Korean defectors who decided to escape North Korea and resettled in South Korea after hearing our broadcasts are precious people who reminded us of the significance of our broadcasting.

In April of 2006, a North Korean spy couple who received orders from the North Korea Worker's Party and had been active in Europe, entered South Korea and visited our station. According to them, they listened to our FNKR broadcast everyday on the internet without missing an airing and it was our broadcasts that played a decisive role in changing their minds. Another time, a high-ranking North Korean elite called via cellphone and expressed his wish to defect; an officer in the North Korean army once sent in materials on public executions, imploring us to tell the outside world of the human rights situation in North Korea.

It has been over 6 years since we started broadcasting into North Korea on internet and over five years on short wave, and during this time FNKR has introduced videos from inside North Korea shot via hidden video cameras 130 times, and FNKR has been quoted more than 90 times by media outlets such as CNN, BBC, and NHK and others regarding our reporting from inside North Korea.

Our 'Voice of the People' program, one of our main programs in which North Korean citizens are interviewed via cellphones, and "News of North Korea from Seoul", are quoted on an almost daily basis by South Korean media outlets such as The Chosun Ilbo and KBS, and even now we still receive a deluge of letters from North Korean citizens who are encouraged by our message of hope.

As a recognition of our achievements FNKR was awarded the 'Media Prize' in December 2008 by Reporters Without Borders, and in December of 2009, we were awarded the 'Asia Democracy and Human Rights Award' by the Taiwan Foundation for Democracy.

However, the achievements of FNKR would have been impossible without the help of the United States Government and the American people. After only three months of starting broadcasts, Free North Korea Radio received funding from the National Endowment for Democracy, and starting from 2006 we have received significant funding from the U.S. State Department's Bureau of Democracy, Human Rights, and Labor.

With these developments in FNKR, there followed many incidents of opposition to the station. First, through their own media outlets, the North Korean regime over twenty times demanded the ceasing of our radio broadcasts, and threatened us by saying "the station that has been instigated by America, the broadcast of turncoats... must be blasted away".

In 2006 and 2007, threatening letters with blood-stained axe and butcher's knife were sent to the station, and in 2009 the person who sent the letter and the packages was found to be receiving orders from the North Korean regime to break up the station, and was arrested by the National Intelligence Service of South Korea, and is now currently in jail.

There are hundreds letters and emails threatening us with death if we do not shut down our station. There are countless happenings of 'press conferences' and 'rallies' demanding our shutdown that have plagued us. The electronic jamming of our broadcasts by the North Korea regime happens on a daily basis, as well as computer hackings of our FNKR website by North Korean agents.

However, we have not ceased broadcasting, not even for a day, since we started FNKR, and the disturbing machinations of the 'enemy' have actually empowered us to continue with our work.

I have received death threats from the North Korea regime from the moment I began this station, to now – the terror threats have continued. That is why I receive 24-hour protection from armed and active-duty police officers. Just this month, on September 6th, my colleague and fellow North Korean defector and activist, Mr. Park Sang Hak of Fighters for Free North Korea, which sends balloons into North Korea, was targeted for assassination; the North Korean spy was discovered and arrested by the South Korean National Intelligence Service.

The efforts of the Kim Jong-il regime to destroy Free North Korea Radio and Fighter for Free North Korea and other North Korean defector groups continue without ceasing. However, we see our work as more valuable than our lives, and that is why we continue our broadcasts and send balloons into North Korea. There is justice in the work we do, and it is the overthrow of the dictatorship regime of Kim Jong-il that is we escaped North Korea in the first place.

Dear Honorable Members of Congress, I truly thank you, the American government, and the American people, for your interest and care for the democratization of North Korea and for its democratic development. Furthermore, I hope for continued international solidarity and cooperation, and I pledge to you that I will continue to devote myself and work for the freedom and liberation of North Korea.

September 20th, 2011
KIM, Seong Min
Free North Korea Radio